Under the Sign of the Lily

The Messianic and Sophianic Age

LIOBANI
I Advise – Do You Accept?

*The Eternal Word,
the One God, the Free Spirit,
speaks through Gabriele,
as through all prophets of God –
Abraham, Job, Moses, Elijah, Isaiah,
Jesus of Nazareth,
the Christ of God*

LIOBANI
I Advise – Do You Accept?

*Explanations and true stories
by LIOBANI, a pure spirit being
from the Eternal Kingdom, revealed
via the prophetess and emissary of God,
Gabriele*

*For children from 6 to 12 years of age
Very rich in teachings for adults, as well*

Gabriele
Publishing House

LIOBANI
I Advise – Do You Accept

1st Edition, June, 2021
© Gabriele-Verlag Das Wort GmbH
Max-Braun-Str. 2, 97828 Marktheidenfeld
www.gabriele-verlag.com
www.gabriele-publishing-house.com

Original German Title:
LIOBANI
Ich berate - nimmst Du an?

The German edition is the work of reference for all
questions regarding the meaning of the contents
Translation authorized by
Gabriele-Verlag Das Wort GmbH

All Rights Reserved

Printed by: KlarDruck GmbH, Marktheidenfeld, Germany

ISBN 978-3-96446-070-7

Contents

For the Parents
Bringing up free, responsible
human beings 9

The Child from Six to Nine Years of Age

Light and shadow in soul and person 23

The invisible beings of thought 26

The incarnations of the soul 28

Only light-filled souls perceive the highest
radiation spheres 30

Everyone has a different state of consciousness 32

The spiritual and the earthly school 38

Become a capable and useful person 45

Whatever you do to your neighbor,
you do to yourself 53

Recognition of abilities and talents, of
difficulties and problems, in good time 56

Raising your child to think positively 60

When parents quarrel 62

Favorite animal and favorite doll 65

A Narrative by Liobani 72

The invisible helpers, the nature beings and
elemental spirits – their path of evolution,
their appearance and activity 72

The air spirits 103

The fire spirits 111

The guardian angels and nature
beings work together 116

The water spirits 121

Home and School 139

Closing the day in the family 139

The morning 150

The school child 154

The law of sowing and reaping 161

The school lessons 187

Games for Training the Senses, Concentration and Self-Recognition 191

A game with the senses 191

A game for training the concentration 199

A game of insight 207

Liobani Continues to Narrate 226

The elemental spirits 226

The forest spirits 236

Elf "Faith Little" reports 237

Sly Fox 244

The little fawn 250

Robin Redbreast 260

The Sun Dance – A prayer dance of the
nature spirits 267

For the Growing Youth From Nine to Twelve Years 279

For the parents 279

Reviewing the book of life 279

Aptitude for a later occupation 283

The growing youth 286
Role model instead of authority 290

For the Young Brothers and Sisters 304
Personal experiences and decisions 304
Abilities, talents, qualities 315
Finding youself 322
Setting a course 329
Selflessness 335
Who is Liobani? – The spirit beings 342
The mountain spirit 353

For the Parents

Bringing up free, responsible human beings

Dear brothers and sisters!

You are enclothed spirit beings and are in an earthly garment for only a short time.

The eternal homeland of all beings is the light of the eternal Father; it is the kingdom of the inner being.

Dear brothers and sisters in the earthly garment, many of you are or will be parents.

The children whom you procreated and gave birth to are, just like you, enclothed spirit beings, children of God.

The man, the father, merely begot the garment, the human being, and the woman, the mother, carries under her heart the developing garment, the growing embryo.

Both, the father, as well as the mother, transferred a part of their hereditary dispositions to the developing earthly body – namely, those parts in the woman, the mother, as well as in the man, the father, that are active during the procreation and time of growth in the mother's womb – they are hereditary factors that may become effective in this life of their child on Earth.

Dear parents, as you have heard, the soul enters the earthly body. In the pure Being, it is a spirit being – just as you and I are spirit beings in the spiritual, divine kingdom.

Insofar as a spirit being has burdened itself, it is called soul. It burdened itself during its incarnations and after leaving its body each time, it went to one of the four soul realms in the spheres of purification. There, the soul returns again and again, until it is purified and has again become a pure spirit being.

Dear parents, when you teach and instruct your child as it takes its first steps in the world, making it aware of many things and situations in this world – always bear in mind that your child also received free will from God.

According to the law of free will, parents are not allowed to repress the will of their child by forcing it to accept their opinions, ideas and habits.

Every person has their own individual soul burden. According to this soul burden, the soul and human being are guided by the planetary constellation to which the soul is connected by having similar vibrations.

Dear parents, please bear in mind that the soul of your child has other burdens, desires, memories and characteristics than your soul – even though some spiritual aspects are similar to the burdens of your soul.

These same or similar burdens have led parents and children together. It is a soul burden, a common karma that links children and parents with one another and that they should bear together.

Remember this when you are teaching a lesson to your often stubborn and disobedient children, so that you do not inhibit their free will by forcing your will upon them. Strive to guide your child, not to dominate it, so that it will become a useful, good, free and happy person.

Dear parents, when your child is disobedient, grumpy and stubborn, don't call the child to order in a commanding way, but guide it! This means, be attentive to the child and find the causes for its behavior. In many cases, the causes lie not only with the child, but also in the way the parents raise their child.

Each day is a "school day," for the adults, as well as for the children, a day on which every single person may recognize their way of thinking and living. And so parents, too, can recognize themselves in the behavior of their children. The children are a mirror for the parents.

The way parents think, the way they live with one another, harmoniously or contentiously, has an effect on their children. Thus, the days on Earth are days of self-recognition, lessons in our earthly garment.

The individual days are shaped by the soul burden of each person and of the child. The day's energy potential flows differently to each person, according to the soul's development and to what the person should deal with today. Therefore, each day is a school day for every human being, for the younger ones as well as for the adults.

At every moment, the energy of the day stimulates a person through their world of thoughts and sensations or through a second or third person. It tells them what they should recognize about themselves, here and now, so that they may clear this up accordingly; either by speaking with someone, through a truly selfless deed, by asking for forgiveness or by forgiving.

The teachers of any one day are the unlawfully applied energies, that is, the negative thoughts, words and actions, with which the person burdened their soul in former incarnations or in the present incarnation – but did not yet clear up.

The same or similarly vibrating energies as the burdened soul carries within itself, also vibrate in the spheres of purification and in the atmosphere. They are attracted by the burdens of the soul according to its activity – we also call these the soul's correspondences. Thus, soul and person are touched each day from within, by their guardian spirit, as well as by like-vibrating energy fields, and thus, a person is guided in such a way, as to daily recognize, at every moment, what should be cleared up today and not first tomorrow.

Therefore, recognize: Each day, God, the eternal law, gives to each person as much recognition and, at the same time, as much strength as is needed to clear up what was recognized, so that the negative energy that has been freed can be transformed into positive, powerful life energy.

If a human being doesn't use the days, the hours, the minutes and seconds of their life, then they are wasting this incarnation. During this incarnation, they could possibly burden themselves with new soul guilt that may be even greater than what they brought into this existence.

Therefore, dear parents, be attentive and recognize that this day is also given to your child as a "school day." You should help your child, so that as an adult, it may be joyful, happy and mostly free of the soul burdens that show their effect on the body.

Please recognize your task – and with this, your responsibility before God; for your child, the spirit being, was beheld, created and given by God and will one day return to God – as you will, too.

Dear parents, many of you know that no energy is lost – not even the transformed-down divine energy that turned into negative energy, because many people have not lived and are not living in a way that is willed by God.

Despite everything, God gives of Himself to His own. He endeavors to help, so that soul and person convert the transformed-down energies back into the positive powers of love, of harmony and peace.

The transformed-down energies remain active until their originator, the soul and the person, recognize themselves and counter the negative – the base, the egocentric – with selfless love, harmony and peace, and devote themselves to the inner light, to Christ, their Redeemer. Christ will then transform the negative into positive, higher vibrating energy.

The light of day brings to each person the causes that should be cleared up today – precisely what is due to be taken care of here and now.

However, the light of day also brings the positive energies for uplifting soul and person and bringing them joy.

Every person receives each day what is good for their soul. In this way, day after day, every person attracts that share of the negative energy of the day created by the person – in former incarnations and during this life on Earth – with negative sensations, thoughts, words and actions, and which is stored in the soul and in the atmosphere.

This will continue to take place until the person recognizes and repents of their mistakes and surrenders them to the Christ-light, the inner light of Redemption. The Spirit of Christ in every soul transforms the negative energies into positive ones, if the person is willing to leave with Christ what has been recognized and for which remorse was felt. Thus, the one who surrenders to the Christ-light the humanness recognized and henceforth refrains from doing it will receive increased positive power.

In addition to the daily energy in the early morning, when the continent gradually turns toward the sun again, from its nightly journey, the soul brings back into its earthly garment the energy potential that soul and person should overcome on this new day and not first tomorrow. On its journey away from the sleeping body and back to it, a part of its burdens is stimulated. This should be recognized by the person on this new day; amends should be made for it and then surrendered to God. The subconscious and the conscious mind also reflect into the new day and, through their world of feelings and thoughts, a person is shown what has to be dealt with today and now.

Consequently, it is possible that on any given day, three energy sources affect the person: the day, the soul, as well as the conscious mind and the subconscious. All three energy sources are attuned to one another by the law of sowing and reaping, so that only so much has to be dealt with today, as is possible for the person. However, the soul also brings joy, harmony and a lot of love into the new day from its nightly journey – as much as corresponds to its sojourn and journey during the night.

When a restless, burdened person sleeps at night, the soul usually stays close to the body. If the person is active at night, then the soul must stay in its human body. In both cases, the soul can attract only a part of the energy of the day through its active correspondences, that is, burdens.

Upon awakening, a person is often assailed by the energy of their day: Sensations and thoughts beset them.

If the person is spiritually aligned, then these daily energies will be given time only after having linked with the highest energy, with God.

If it is possible for a person to put order in the human sensations and thoughts – the negativity from the personal energy of the day that comes up already in the morning – and they can be given over to God, the primordial energy, while asking for guidance in the new day, then the day will be under the positive forces of God.

Then, the God-conscious person will be guided by the divine energies in such a way that, despite possible difficulties, the energy of the day brings a positive result – because the person recognized the positive in the negative and gave it room to take effect.

A person whose soul is filled with light for the most part and whose conscious mind and subconscious are clear, will be guided day after day by the indwelling divine power in such a way that the still-existing shortcomings and difficulties will be recognized in good time, and they will be solved and cleared up with the help of the divine power. Then, the days will be largely harmonious and balanced. Many a difficulty will be solved in a positive sense, because in the person's soul these or similar difficulties hardly vibrate anymore or no longer exist.

Difficulties that the day brings for an individual can also be the difficulties of a group.

This means that a group of people has burdened itself with the same or similar feelings, thoughts and actions and projected these energies into the atmosphere. If these energies become active, then the individual can come in contact with them, perhaps together with other people.

Dear parents, please heed this section about the energy of the day. With it, you gain understanding for your child, which likewise attracts its daily potential of positive and negative energy.

But don't excuse things right away by saying: "That was the child's energy of the day," when for example, it pouts today and is not at all open, when it cries a lot and is moody or even quarrelsome and destructive. But ask yourselves the question whether you, dear parents, were cranky and moody in the past few days, whether you quarreled with one another or talked about people, things and situations that your child was not able to deal with and understand. This still-vibrating energy complex, which is fading away, is then active in your child's conscious mind and subconscious and determines its day.

Dear parents, do not force your will on your child. Guide your child as you would like to be guided: Not in a straitjacket of human ideas, not in the armor of traditions and inherited thought, like, for example: "Since our ancestors acted this way, our children also have to do it this way."

Think about it: Every person has their own individual life, shaped by their own body of thought.

Parents have the task – and the obligation! – to take care of their children, to protect and raise them to be independent and just in their thinking, speaking and acting, so that they become spiritually alert and active adults who master their lives and are in harmony with their fellow people.

Alert spiritual people see things and events in the world as they are, not as they are seen through the glasses of a worldly person, who, from childhood on, has worn the confining straitjacket and the armor of ideas and traditions of their ancestors and parents.

Raise your children to be free people! Be a living example, so that they affirm your good words of advice, accept them and perhaps put them into practice, if these correspond to their life rhythm.

If your children are not willing to accept your recognitions and advice, then leave them in their mindset and with their wishes. However, remain loving and kindly disposed toward them.

Please don't talk insistently to them until they become resigned and say "yes" and do what you want. In that way, you merely seem to have achieved something. Sooner or later they will become stubborn and will reject both or one of their parents.

Dear parents, your life is not the life of your child.

Your child has the right to develop freely, to be cared for, protected and guided correctly, that is, with composure, by its parents.

If parents and family are in harmony, if there is trust and selfless love among them, the parents will lead their child through its childhood in an understanding way.

Dear parents, the way you think and live, that is how you will influence and go toward your children.

If you as parents, or one of you, are dominating, that is, authoritarian, then your children are not able to develop freely and the negative genetic dispositions you have transmitted to their physical bodies begin to develop more rapidly and increase in intensity. These then become more strongly evident in the children and cover up the positive sides, their inner values.

The active, negative hereditary dispositions can affect the burdens of the soul, intensify and shape the daily events of your growing child in a bleak and painful way. They may influence the youth and the adult, who then becomes an imitator of the parents, who has no world of feelings and thoughts of their own, but is a marionette of the parents as a result of an authoritarian upbringing.

Please, dear parents, do not raise your children in an authoritarian way, but be authorities, positive role models!

The authoritarian is rigid and a know-it-all.

The authority is a good example, is understanding, tolerant, well-disposed, forgiving and kind.

People who have been shaped by their parents and hardly know themselves may have to suffer a lot, because they are unable to recognize, sort and deal with what the day brings them, their personal energy of the day. They are being "lived" by their ancestors and parents, which means that the worldview held by their ancestors and parents, their body of thought and traditions and much more, has been forced upon them.

In this way, their development is inhibited, and it is often very difficult for them to find their way out of the straitjacket and the armor of ideas and opinions of others, since their entire thinking and living until now has been shaped by them. Such people were and are lived by the daily energies of others. They are not themselves. They are the result of the desires and ideas of the body of thought of their ancestors and parents.

Such people pass their own life by. They don't really perceive the opportunity of their incarnation and don't make use of it, but instead, build up a group karma with their parents that they will have to expiate together, either in this or in one of their next lives.

The parents have burdened themselves more strongly with this, because they forced their world of concepts upon their child and did not guide the child into its own development.

As a result, the youth or later the adult burdens themselves with wrong thinking and acting, which can be attributed to an improper upbringing. In addition, there is their own soul burden, which they could not recognize because they persisted in the straitjacket and armor of their parents' human thinking and wanting.

The correct attitude toward life for parents as well as for children would be: One is a mirror for the other; the one recognizes itself in the other, and each one helps to carry the burden of the other.

This makes a person free and leads to selfless love, not to an authoritarian behavior, but to a true role model. That is a true Christian communal life.

A genuine living community means: Support one another and fulfill the laws of the Eternal.

The adult person will be touched and guided by God's law itself. In many cases, the child will be guided by God by way of its parents. Consequently, parents have taken on a great and high task for their children.

God strives to guide His human child again and again in such a way that it can let go of its old habits and take off the straitjacket and burst the armor of the human ego, the ideas and traditions.

The one who knows how to correctly use the laws of God each day will gradually turn to the Inner Path. It leads to the liberation from the human ego and to the unity with God who created His child, the spirit being, as a free child and who repeatedly gives it the opportunity to live in Him and to go through the day with Him as his day.

The Child from Six to Nine Years of Age

Dear child, you, who are my sister or my brother! My name is Liobani, a divine being who wants to offer you some advice on your further journey through life.

Yes, you understood correctly, I merely want to advise you and not to order or even command you to do something that you don't recognize or don't want to do.

You see my child, I am a free being of heaven and therefore, am not tied to any human desires or opinion.

Light and shadow in soul and person

You, too, will again be a free heavenly being, because God gave you the strength to refine your human senses, your senses of sight, of hearing, smell, taste and touch, in such a way that your soul will again be able to see its homeland, to hear God and the beings of love again, to smell the divine fragrances, to again be able to taste the fine ethereal substances in naturally produced foods and also be able to touch the forms of life consciously, that is, in the knowledge that everything is life.

Surely you will now ask your parents the question: What are the senses and how do they work? I would like to explain this to you:

Through your feelings, thoughts, words and actions, the world of your senses shows the light and shadowed sides in your life.

Light and shadow are in your soul, as well as in your earthly body. They form your consciousness now.

Your brain cells absorb what you felt and thought yesterday, what you are feeling and thinking today and now; they reflect these sensations and thoughts into the soul. From there, light and shadow have an effect on your sensory organs and, in turn, on your feelings, thoughts, words and actions.

You must recognize that one thing has an effect on another: Your feelings and thoughts have an effect on your senses, and your senses, in turn, stimulate your feelings and thoughts. Light and shadow, your senses, your feeling, thinking, speaking and acting, direct your eyes; these have an effect on your senses of hearing, smell, taste and touch. What you desire in the way of food, fragrances and odors directs the smelling membranes in your nose; they also have an effect on your palate, for your organs of smell and taste are very close together.

Everything that you have felt, thought, said and done until now has an effect on your soul and on your brain as light or shadow. Conversely, everything that is stored in the soul or in the brain – even what is unconscious, what you seem to have already forgotten – likewise stimulates, in turn, your senses, feelings and thoughts.

As long as your feelings and thoughts are not selfless, that is, loving, helpful and of good will, you are controlled by the shadows of your soul. If the shadows of your soul, the burdens of your soul, are very great, then you will be driven, so to speak. Then, in many cases, you are no longer the master of your senses. The shadows of your soul express themselves, for example, in fear, hatred, envy, anger.

On the other hand, the light in your soul and in your brain cells wants to guide you and makes an effort, to help you become free from this dependency on your senses and on your negative feelings, thoughts, words and actions, that is, free from the shadows, in order to then live in the light.

If your feelings and thoughts are loving, then your true being will gradually look through your physical eyes, the spirit being that you were in heaven and that now lives on the Earth as a soul in an earthly body, in order to again become like an angel, that is, free and pure.

If your soul is light-filled and bright, then your senses will no longer be driven by the many human desires, by envy, hatred and quarrelsome thoughts, but rather, your five senses will react to finer spheres of radiation. For example, your curiosity will decrease; you will meet with children who have the same or similar radiation sphere as you do – who, like you, also want to peacefully live, play and do their schoolwork with the playmates, classmates and brothers and sisters who are loving to their brothers and sisters.

The invisible beings of thought

The senses can also be compared to small antennas or feelers. I remind you of a snail. When a snail feels that there is danger, then it pulls in its feelers, which are its antennas. The snail senses with its feelers what is before it and thus, perceives its surroundings.

It is similar with human beings.

If a person's soul has a lot of light and if their thoughts are loving, then the person will direct light-filled and pure thoughts and feelings to their self and the senses will likewise attract light-filled people.

Feelings, sensations and thoughts can be compared to small beings, also called the invisible thought beings. They vibrate in the Earth's atmosphere and on the Earth and are attracted by the senses of that person who sends out corresponding, that is, light-filled, loving thoughts and words and whose actions are good.

The same applies when a person is unkind, hateful and angry. Then, with the senses, they attract small, invisible, unkind, hateful and angry thought beings. The light-filled as well as the dark thought beings are taken in by the antennas, the senses, of a person, according to the nature of the soul in the person.

Thus, the invisible thought beings have an effect on people's body and soul, whether they are standing in the light or in shadows, whether they have light or shadow in their soul: Light-filled thought beings have an effect on light-filled people and souls; dark thought beings have an effect on souls that are poor in light and rich in shadows, as well as on dismal-thinking people. That's why it is said: What a person thinks and speaks, that is what they are.

As it is with all animals, the snail is not shadowed. According to its life form, it feels in a light-filled way, that means, its delicate sensations are pure, creative love.

Creative love, feelings of love, are feelings of unity. The snail and all animals are in unity with nature.

The snail, which is in harmony with creation, immediately pulls in its feelers when it registers disharmonious vibrations. They mean danger for it. In this way, it protects itself from danger. A light-filled person who feels and thinks lovingly will act similarly to the snail: When ugly and unloving words are spoken, for example, when people are being disparaged or even talked about maliciously, then a light-filled person closes their senses to these negative, disharmonious vibrations. They do not allow these dark thought beings, these negative forces, into their light-filled soul and into their brain cells, which are attuned to goodness. They protect themselves against them by keeping the antennas of their senses aligned with the Father's love, with the power that is active in their soul, in every cell of their body, but also in the tree, in the leaf, in each flower, in the bush and in every animal. This one life force is active in each person, in every heavenly body and in all of infinity.

The incarnations of the soul

Dear child, when I speak of life, I do not mean only your present life on Earth, but all your lives on Earth, because in the alternation of birth and death, a soul seeks out a new human body again and again, that is, it repeatedly incarnates into a new physical body.

Your soul, which lives in your physical body, goes into other radiation spheres after the death of this body.

If it is very burdened, that is, if its shadows are very dense, then it will come to Earth again and enter a body. This can happen many times, until soul and person have lightened the dense shadows, therefore, until the soul has become brighter again.

At the birth of a child, the soul, the spirit body, slips into the physical body, into the infant. A person cannot see this process, because the soul cannot be perceived with human eyes.

When the physical body, the human being, dies, then the soul leaves the dead body. It is imbedded in the Spirit of our eternal Father, who is the life of the soul and of the body. As I have already mentioned, the soul then goes to other radiation spheres, where other souls live according to their soul's condition, either to light or to dark soul realms.

A shadowed soul goes to where those souls live that are shadowed to the same or similar extent as the arriving soul, which has just left its dead body. Light-filled souls likewise go to light-filled souls. According to the law of attraction, this means that dark souls go to dark souls and light-filled souls, to light-filled souls.

Souls with great burdens, with dense shadows, often press to incarnate in an earthly body. Many of these densely shadowed souls again long for a human body, because they believe that the Earth and the human body are their true home.

The life on Earth is the spiritual school of souls. Someone who is friendly, loving and understanding in the spiritual school lightens their shadows and their soul will become more light-filled and brighter. This takes place when a person recognizes the outbursts of anger and the spite as a part of themselves and then surrenders such ugly, human thought beings to the heavenly Father, with the request for help not to be angry and bad again. If the person can conquer their ego, then they will feel, think, speak and act in a friendlier, kinder and more understanding way. If it is good for their already bright soul, it will not have to come back to Earth into a human body after death; instead, in light-filled radiation spheres, it will continue to strive to become ever more selfless and loving until it has again become angel-like.

Once the soul has become totally bright and filled with light, once there are no more shadows on it, then it is an angel again, as pure as the angels in heaven are, and as pure as I, an angel of heaven, also am.

Only light-filled souls perceive the highest radiation spheres

Surely you are interested in why you cannot see or hear me.

I will answer you: You see, dear child, I live in fine, heavenly, light-filled radiation spheres. These radiation spheres cannot be seen with human eyes. Thus, you are not able to see me, either.

And you will be able to hear me only once you are again closer to an angel-like consciousness; for like connects only with like.

You have heard of the five senses that are like antennas. When the feelings and thoughts of the human being are filled with light, when the senses are refined and aligned with the highest radiation spheres, then the person feels and thinks in a friendly, good and loving way. Their words connect and do not divide.

If the feeling and thinking of the human being are light-filled, friendly and loving, then their actions will also be good, that is, selfless. Such a person does not expect thanks or acknowledgment for what they do. This shows that their senses are fine and are aligned with the highest radiation spheres. For such a person, it is possible to experience God, our Father, in the light-filled soul, as well as the light-filled beings that live in the heavenly radiation spheres.

However, so that you can receive my message with your human senses, I use the language of a person, who is called the emissary of God and prophetess of Christ. She is your sister, called Gabriele on Earth.

The radiation spheres of which you have heard are very fine vibrations of love or streams of love, which cannot be seen by the human eye and cannot be perceived with the human ear.

Our sister Gabriele, however, can hear me in her light-filled soul, because she has aligned her fine senses with the highest radiation spheres, the fine vibrations of love. She has also seen me in a fine radiation sphere in the kingdom of the innermost being. From there, I transmitted to her the body exercises for adults and for the youth. She tried to imitate these body exercises in order to pass them on to her human brothers and sisters. In this way, the body exercises came into the material radiation spheres, that is, to this Earth and into this world.

Therefore, there are also material radiation spheres. They consist of innumerable vibrations. They form the consciousness of humankind.

The whole earthly radiation network together is called the material radiation sphere. Every person has a different state of consciousness and everyone radiates according to their feelings, thoughts, words and actions.

Everyone has a different state of consciousness

ou will surely ask the question what is consciousness or state of consciousness.

I, Liobani, would like to explain this to you: The spiritual consciousness is in the soul. It is what the soul and person have already actualized.

Actualization means: To transform the ugly and the loveless into the good and pure. This means that, again and again, the person surrenders the bad thoughts of fear, envy, anger, rage and unkind words to the Spirit of Christ in the innermost part of their soul. The Spirit of Christ in you will then transform into fine vibrations all that is human in you in the way of envy, anger, hate, greed, rage and everything that you surrender to Him and leave with Him. Then, you will be tolerant and warmhearted, loving and understanding. So that is actualization: The coarse, grim vibrations like envy, hatred, anger are transformed into fine vibrations of good will, kindness and selfless love; then, you have become good and loving.

An example: Suddenly, anger against your brother rises in you. You realize that you are angry only because your brother has a toy car that you would like to have, but you did not get it. If you then pause for a moment and tell yourself: "No I mustn't be envious or angry. It belongs to my brother and from my heart I do not begrudge it him," then you feel remorse for your fit of anger. In the evening, you can then surrender your anger to your heavenly Father in prayer, asking Him: "Father, please make everything good again." And if you can say to your brother the next day: "Yesterday I wanted your car. I was really mad at you, because you had it and I did not get it," then you have regretted what you did. And what has been regretted will be transformed into fine vibrations!

Then, you can say to your brother: "Today I am very glad that you have this toy car and that I can tell you that. I really like you, please forgive me because I wasn't good."

And when everything is good again and the clouds of anger have disappeared, since our heavenly Father has transformed them into vibrations of light and love, then it will be brighter in your soul. This means that your consciousness will expand, that is, your soul will be more light-filled.

The state of consciousness is the state or condition of each individual person. The word "state" says the following: In spirit, you are where you have put yourselves: either with children who are angry, envious, loveless and quarrelsome – as you, too, are – or with children who endeavor to be good to their brothers and sisters and to their playmates, who endeavor to play together and be friendly to one another – as you do, as well.

Every person is attracted by those people who think and feel in a similar or same way as they do, and every

person attracts, in turn, people who feel, think, talk and act as they do. The spiritual law of attraction, namely, brings about the fact that like attracts like.

Thus, your state of consciousness corresponds to your feelings and thoughts, to your words and actions, to your warm-heartedness or to your lack of love.

If you are with children who think in the same or similar way, either warmhearted or angry, then this is your and their state of consciousness.

The way a person thinks, talks and acts is the way their character is – this applies to you, too. That is your and their state of consciousness.

During the course of your growth and in your maturing years, you will recognize that every person thinks and speaks differently, and that no person is exactly like another. This is also true for the consciousness, the character, of your neighbor. Each one has their own state of consciousness and therefore, a different character.

Dear brothers and sisters, because each person has their own state of consciousness and therefore, hears and understands my words, what I have revealed, differently and because each person has received from God the free will to decide – and thus, can choose whether they want to believe and accept what is said or not – that is why I will merely advise you and your parents. I will explain to them and to you the eternal laws of our heavenly

Father. Whether your parents and you follow them, I leave that up to your parents and to you, as well.

You now know: All spirit beings, souls and also people have received their free will from God. The free will is part of the absolute, universal law. It is untouchable, inviolable. That means, that neither spirit beings nor souls nor human beings can change it in any way.

Your parents and you, too, decide whether you accept the laws of the eternal Father and want to put them into practice in daily life or not.

I merely offer advice.

According to divine love, free will is the highest good.

It leads the person to inner spiritual freedom. It allows those who aspire to God to recognize the truth and leads soul and person to the divine wisdom.

The divine love is the sustainer of the free will and of wisdom.

The one who loves their neighbor selflessly without expecting anything from them, and who doesn't boss their fellow people around looks deeper into the divine events. This person becomes a knowing and wise person, who selflessly loves all beings – human beings and all forms of life like plants, animals, stones and stars – because of recognizing God's love and His ruling hand in all things.

You may want to ask me what it means to look into the divine events.

You must know that God reveals Himself at every moment. Usually, you don't notice this, because your senses are wandering around uncontrolled. However, when you know, that is, when you are aware, that every flower, every blade of grass, every leaf, every animal, stone and every ray of the sun is an expression of the divine power, then you will gradually sense the divine workings with your spiritual senses. You will acknowledge this and you will admire the diversity of God in amazement – and then you will learn to love God, our Father, who has given us the essence of infinity.

When a leaf moves in the wind, for example, this, too, is a divine occurrence, a process that was triggered by the Spirit of your heavenly Father. The presence of the Father, His breath of life, His Spirit, is in the leaf and in the wind. When you look at the stars, then you should know that they are also divine powers, the works of God.

The Spirit of the Father is light and power; it is the Father's love that shows and reveals itself in this world in many ways.

Nothing that God created is rigid. Everything is movement, because the divine power is always active.

Everything that lives bears within the Spirit of God, the life.

The one who acknowledges the pure and the beautiful in God, our Father, as His power looks ever more deeply into the workings of God, our beloved, heavenly Father.

The spiritual and the earthly school

Dear child, there are still many things to tell, but I would like to gradually come to my task: to offer you and your parents advice – will you accept it?

In addition to the explanations of the divine laws, I will, however, also tell you again and again about the life in the eternal homeland, which is our true home.

Dear child, you are on Earth in order to lighten your soul burdens more and more, the shadows of your spirit body, which lives in your earthly body. You should dissolve the shadows with light-filled feelings, thoughts, words and with active, spiritual, selfless actions.

Then, instead of the shadows, bright, radiating divine light will shine. Then, you will have expanded your consciousness and in this way, you will also be closer to God, our heavenly Father.

On Earth you are in a spiritual school.

During your life on Earth, on the way to the heavenly Father's house, you learn how a person should think, speak and act divinely, that is, how they should live. That is the spiritual school for all people. Each day, you receive smaller and larger tasks from God, your Father. They are given to you by God and by your guardian angel according to your age on Earth. The Spirit of our heavenly Father and your guardian angel help you to fulfill and put into practice what you have recognized.

For example, when you are angry, then your conscience says: "The way you are now thinking and speaking is not good. You are angry, because you did not get this or that. That is not good." Or you are angry, because your brother or sister gave an answer to your question that you did not want to hear. Your conscience asks you: "Why didn't you want to hear this answer?" Or if you don't want to go to bed, or someone even hit you, then ask yourself: "Why did this happen?" When you react angrily, this always has one or more reasons. If you have found them, then you know what is happening inside you. The conscience is either the Spirit of your Father in you, for you are the house, the temple, in which the Spirit of our heavenly Father dwells, or it is your invisible guide, your guardian angel, who admonishes you.

Dear child, you have heard that like always attract like. This is why nothing in life happens by chance.

If two like-vibrating, ugly and bad thoughts come together, then the result is like an explosion: The person is angry: they explode and speak ugly words or strike out.

So when you are angry, you send out ugly and unkind thought-beings. And with words, you release more negative energy.

Your fit of anger may have occurred because the shadows of your soul attracted what your neighbor sent out.

Therefore, the fit of anger was triggered not only by your friends. Through their behavior, they touched the shadow of your soul. This shadow began to vibrate more strongly and broke out in you as anger.

Before this outburst, during and after your anger, the Spirit of your heavenly Father and your guardian angel endeavored, and continue to endeavor, to enlighten you with the following love-sensations:

"Dear child, first look at yourself before you blame your friend or your supposed enemy in your anger. Look at yourself, whether you aren't still expecting something from them – or whether you are angry because they did not give you the answer that you wanted to hear. Perhaps you wanted to be flattered?"

Or if your friend or your supposed enemy has hit you, ask yourself, how did you behave, what thoughts did you have toward your neighbor, your friend or apparent enemy. Were your thoughts loving or hateful? Therefore, look for the shadows in yourself and not in your friend or apparent enemy.

See, dear little brother or sister, that is the school of life of our heavenly Father for His earthly children. The Spirit of our heavenly Father and our guardian angel admonish, help and protect, according to the behavior of the child. The instructions for our life from our heavenly Father and our guardian angel are very comprehensive.

It is possible that there are several shadows in your soul, which the Spirit of your heavenly Father and your guardian angel want to lighten together with you, so that your soul becomes more light-filled and brighter. Thus, if you pay attention to your conscience and follow the good and loving sensations and thoughts – or you pay attention to the loving words and admonishments of your parents, who have also been chosen by God for you to protect you, to take care of you, to help you and to guide you on your way into becoming a teenager and an adult – thus, if you are obedient, which doesn't mean submissive, and your parents protect you, take care of you and guide you according to the laws of selfless love, then you are in the best of care.

God, your guardian angel and your parents take care of you.

Therefore, you receive a lot of help in the spiritual school of life. Your grandparents and your relatives can also give you many a good piece of advice.

Aside from all this selfless care, you will also visit the worldly school, in which you can develop your spiritual and human abilities.

According to the law of God, the following sentence applies to everyone: "Live in order to learn" – and not: "Learn in order to live."

Let your father explain this sentence to you. He surely knows what it means.

Dear school child, you are now taking the first step into the world: You are starting school.

When a child has reached a certain age, then it has to visit an earthly school according to the laws of your country.

Why must six- or seven-year-old children go to the earthly school? One reason is because people should use their spiritual capabilities during their life on Earth. And another reason is that a person should learn to correctly apply the law "pray and work" and put it into practice.

Although you are in a spiritual school, the worldly school is also necessary, because as a human child you also need material bread and other material things.

What a person needs, they have to work for, again, with God's power. Whatever a person accomplishes, they are able to do it only through the indwelling power, the Spirit of the Father in the person's soul.

Therefore, you may not to refuse to attend this earthly school. You can certainly say: "I don't like this learning material; I would like to learn something else." But if this material has been prescribed by the school, you will simply have to comply.

The learning material is set for each school class respectively, and the teachers have to teach their pupils this learning material and to make efforts, so that the pupils also understand the respective subject matter.

Thus, you cannot hold the teacher responsible for what you have to learn. You should also come to terms with this situation.

How can you come to terms with the situation in the quickest way?

If during the lesson hours, you apply correctly everything that you have learned in the spiritual school until now, then it will be much easier for you to join in the lessons and also to understand your teachers. Your teachers are your brother or sister in the spirit. They endeavor to teach you the educational material, so that you learn to correctly express yourself in this world and can understand what is necessary for this life on Earth.

The first school day will certainly bring you great joy.

Perhaps you received a new dress or a new pullover, a new jacket or a new coat. Or your school bag is either new or has been freshly refurbished, if it was handed down from one of your brothers and sisters. On the first day of school, either your father or your mother, or both, will accompany you.

Your parents who, themselves, successfully learn and actualize in the spiritual school, in order to become angel-like again, will instruct you and tell you how you should behave toward your schoolmates according to the divine laws, so that you are able to live with them in peace. They will also advise you to confide in your teacher when you have difficulties. And they will explain to you why you should respect your teacher. They make an effort to convey to you the first school knowledge and tasks.

You will surely ask why you have to go to the worldly school, when there is the spiritual one.

Dear school child, understand the difference between the two terms "spiritual school" and "earthly school":

In the spiritual school, you learn how you can free your soul from its shadows.

In the earthly school, you learn how to draw, to read and write and how to do arithmetic. You learn local history, about nature and geography and in social studies, you learn which rules and laws the citizens of this earthly country should live by. In your further studies, you learn history and the history of art. In this earthly school, your practical abilities and talents will also be awakened.

The school lessons will not be all-too-difficult for you, if you make efforts to correctly apply all that you have learned in the spiritual school until now, for the divine laws of our heavenly Father should also be heeded and applied in the world, in the earthly school.

Become a capable and useful person

The human body has many, many cells, and every cell of your body is in constant vibration, in constant action and reaction. Your body cells need healthy and sustaining food every day. Your brain cells need food and training.

When your teachers instruct you and teach you how to learn, it is correct, so that you become a capable and useful person once you are a teenager or an adult. So it is necessary to affirm what the teachers say.

However, "capable" and "useful" are flexible words. So that you can understand what this expression "flexible word" means, I remind you of a rubber band. You can say about a rubber band: "It is too short." If you pull on the rubber band, then you say: "It is long."

Dear school child, so the statement of educators "You should become a capable and useful person" is also a flexible statement. Think about the comparison with the rubber band!

A person is good and kind and truly wise only when they bring the worldly laws into accord with the divine laws.

But if the teachers think only of a person's school education, then they are shortsighted. They are being shortsighted for the overriding truth, for the divine laws, because they believe that a person is capable and useful in the world only when they fill up their brain cells with a lot of human knowledge, with opinions and theories, so that they can work correctly and well in the world and are useful people.

People who see this life on Earth as their true life and acknowledge only the Earth as their true home are limited people.

Limited means, they are shortsighted. Their view is narrow. They have a so-called "narrow-minded" way of thinking. This means: They follow only one goal, of which they believe that it is good for themselves and for people who think and live as they do. Such people believe only what they can hear and see, and they reject what cannot be recognized and figured out at first sight.

The divine truth will remain hidden from a person and covered up by the shadows, the burdens of their soul, until a person recognizes the purpose of their life on Earth and strives for higher ideals and values. At first, these are to be found only in them.

Shortsightedness, which doesn't look beyond worldly knowledge and things, makes many people arrogant and self-centered. In the long run, such people become envious, quarrelsome and pugnacious, because they are only intent on defending their opinion and their small, human ego, their narrow-minded thinking and human beliefs.

They desperately want to be right and, therefore, with all means and methods available to them, they fight against those people who do not share their viewpoints. They fight with thoughts of hatred and envy – and perhaps even make false statements in order to exalt themselves, their ego.

Through such wrong behavior, fighting and hatred has come and continues to come into this world. Animosity and envy have developed and continue to develop from this.

Human beings must change themselves so that peace, hope and confidence can come into this world.

People should be caring and not bind others through hatred, envy, fighting and by being self-opinionated.

Those who want to bind their neighbor to themselves with these human aspects and force them to think and to do what they think is right sow discord.

This discord causes unfriendliness and unkindness, that is, the division into thine and mine.

Those who are focused on themselves isolate themselves from all others instead of connecting with them. This is not selfless love for your neighbor.

Know, dear growing young person, that even unfriendly and loveless looks at another person can cause a lot of harm!

Often, the one wants to have what the other has, and if they cannot have it, no matter for what reason, they become envious and intolerant.

Those who are intolerant deny their neighbor much, but attribute much to themselves, that is, they exalt themselves. For example, when they are upset, they talk about their neighbors and accuse them of being stupid, lazy or dishonest. They think they know everything better and are smarter than their fellow people.

With their agitation and by the way they speak, such people show us what they think. And what people think is what they are! Not only the other person, to whom they attribute all this is this way, but also those who, in their agitation, have said bad and hateful things. That is unkind and intolerant, never noble and spiritual.

People who by nature are short-sighted and who disparage others have serious problems and worries, because they have not accomplished what they wanted to in their lives or because their neighbor thinks and acts differently than they want.

With this, the person's thoughts are too preoccupied with their neighbor, instead of with the events of the day; thus, they are "absent-minded" or even brood over their own worries and problems.

In this way, they drown out their conscience and possibly fail to recognize a danger that lies in wait, because they do not have themselves under control and are not concentrated.

Accidents and blows of fate are the result of such behavior patterns. Illness and, at times, severe suffering can be the result.

You have heard: When the shadows in the soul, the burdens, radiate more strongly or when they are triggered externally by some kind of incident or other, with words, pictures or something else, then parts of the shadows in the soul begin to vibrate and the person attracts what vibrates in a similar way to the person. For example, when two people heatedly argue with one another, then the shadows of the soul vibrate not only in one of them, but in both. Similar soul-shadows, also called vibrations, come into conflict; thereby, vehemence and contention are triggered and an explosive kind of altercation develops.

Therefore, you can see that whatever lies in the soul expresses itself externally!

If the soul-shadow penetrates the body more strongly, it becomes effective there as illness; this means, the person becomes ill. You know that all these shadows were inflicted upon the inner body, the spirit body, the soul, through the wrong behavior of the person – either in a former life or in this existence.

You have already learned that the soul in the human being is on Earth to become divine again, to discard its shadows in a law-abiding, selfless life of love, according to the will of God.

You are now a pupil. If pupils merely collect one-sided knowledge and strive to be someone important in the world and attain prestige, then, in reality, they are small, for they have not included the spiritual life in their thinking and living. Their orientation is one-sided and because they see all things and occurrences from their point of view, namely, from the world, from the material point of view, they become self-opinionated. Consequently, their spiritual consciousness remains small; they live past the truth and therefore, cannot include the divine in their thoughts and actions.

People who are only worldly-oriented seldom think of their soul's shadows, of their soul burdens, which can break open either already today or tomorrow, or only in a few years or in another life on Earth; these then often destroy everything that the person has laboriously acquired, for example, because of their greed. A blow of fate can suddenly, unexpectedly, confine a distinguished person to their sickbed, or, because of some circumstance or other, they lose all their possessions and property or their good job.

The Earth is a place of residence for beggars and kings, for rich and poor. The blows of fate in this world are multifaceted and diverse, so it can rightly be said that the Earth is a vale of tears for most people.

Beggars and kings, rich and poor, are on this Earth to clear up and overcome what they have caused and want to make amends for, or also to serve and help their neighbor.

Dear growing young person, many things would not have to be in this world.

If people would heed the spiritual school of life and entrust their lives to God, if they would live by the divine laws and bring their life and their work on Earth into accord with the divine laws, then there would be less and less envy, hatred, quarreling, animosity, wars or problems, hardship and illness among the people. People would be friendlier and more loving to one another and the one would support the other.

Dear child, you should become a capable person who also has success in the world through honesty, integrity and selfless love. A person who does not see their success as their own merit, but know that God's love and wisdom have led them to success – perhaps also in order to support smaller brothers and sisters, as you still are, with love and understanding. In this way, they, too, can grow up in the Spirit, in selfless love and become good, diligent adults whose orientation is not one-sided, not self-centered, but who are there for all people who put the common good before their own well-being.

Selflessness serves the common good and the common good leads to unity with God and with all people.

Unity with God and with all people brings about, in turn, selfless love, freedom, greatness and good will toward all people.

If you want to become a great, spiritual person, who is wise, who integrates the spiritual, divine law, the love of our heavenly Father into their life on Earth, into their thinking, speaking and acting – then accept and put into practice what I will now explain further to you.

Your guardian angel, whom your heavenly Father placed at your side, helps you to put your thoughts in order and to attune them with the good, noble and fine.

According to the eternal law, it also supports you when you go to school and do your homework. It helps you when you are playing. In every situation in life, your good, invisible friend, your companion, your guardian angel, helps you.

So that your guardian angel can reach you with its loving and admonishing words, which are fine vibrations, you should build a bridge of thought to it: This bridge consists of your selfless thoughts of love, of friendship and of a correct understanding toward your parents, grandparents, relatives, teachers, schoolmates, your own brothers and sisters and all people – no matter who they are, what they look like or what they think and say.

Whoever feels, thinks and lives in this way has God's help and the help of their guardian angel. They are very closely linked with their guardian angel, their invisible friend.

Whatever you do to your neighbor, you do to yourself

Dear school child, once again, you have the hours at school behind you. They were perhaps strenuous, because you were very attentive; you concentrated and worked well. You are going home now.

On the way home to your parent's house, you already begin to relax: to skip, laugh and be happy. Play along when your schoolmates are playing some game or other, even if it is merely making funny faces or clowning around by hopping from one foot to the other and laughing out loud or pushing up your cheeks and squeezing your eyes together, so that the world looks very small.

But don't forget to watch out for traffic and for other pedestrians; they are your fellow people. Do not bump into them in your high spirits and do not hinder them in some way or other. You certainly do not want to be pushed or even hindered on your way to school because of someone else's lack of attention.

Remember this sentence: "Do not do to others what you do not want done to you."

Who is the other one?

It is your neighbor. It is all people, big and small, older and younger.

Know that the spirit body in a person is always young, because it has eternal life. Only the shell, the human being, withers during the years on Earth.

The spiritual body possesses eternal life. Only the shell decays, that is, the person, the flesh and bones. The soul journeys back to God step by step, according to the way the person thinks and lives.

Who is your neighbor?

All people are your neighbors: your parents, your grandparents, relatives, teachers, your own brothers and sisters and your school friends; not only your friend is your neighbor, but also the one who is against you.

God's love is the eternal law. It is active in every soul and in every human being, in all of infinity.

Since in every person God's same love, the law, is active, that is why your neighbor is also a part of you. Everything pure, God's love, the same power of love, is contained in all things. That is why every being is a part of God's love, likewise your neighbor, just like you.

If you now hate your neighbor, quarrel with them, or think and speak about your neighbor in an unfriendly and unloving way, then you will not diminish the heavenly Father's power of love in your neighbor, about whom you think and speak unlovingly; nor will you blow out the light of love in their soul. Oh no! You diminish the light, the

heavenly Father's power of love, in yourself, in your own soul. Consequently, the shadows become denser and bigger in your own soul.

Since everything is contained in all things, the law of love says: "Whatever you do to your neighbor, you do to yourself."

Therefore, with your unkind behavior, you diminish the divine light, the power of love, in yourself and the shadows of your soul become bigger.

Therefore, my child, be mindful of this.

Recognition of abilities and talents, of difficulties and problems, in good time

ou now come home from school to your parents' house. You walk into the house or apartment.

How does a polite, well brought-up spirit child, which goes to the spiritual, as well as to the worldly school, behave?

Greet your parents and your siblings in a friendly and heartfelt way.

Surely your mother has prepared a snack for you, or perhaps you are just in time for lunch: Make it a habit to thank God for the food, for His gift of love, whether it is a snack or lunch.

You have heard from me that everything that lives is God, the power, the love.

On the way home from school, you practice seeing the people, plants, animals and stones, everything, as a living expression of God.

The life from God is also in your food. For this reason, thank your eternal Father, who loves you.

At every moment, God shows the people that He loves them. Through His Spirit, He gives of Himself. This spirit is life, that is, energy, in your food, as well as in the water, in the air and in the fire.

So be thankful and be happy about your food and drink, about the gifts from God, of which you now partake.

Eat consciously. This means: Do not talk while you eat. Do not drink when your mouth is still full of food. Do not eat too fast, but calmly and be glad that it tastes good.

Once you have eaten, thank the Father for His gifts of love, which now strengthen your body. Give thanks that you have again gained strength.

You will now rest for a while in your room or play or maybe do your homework right away. You can decide for yourself what you would like to do first.

Dear parents, some good advice from Liobani:

When your child comes home, don't assail it with questions, how school was and what tasks need to be done today.

Endeavor to show your child that you respect its will and regard it as a spiritually mature person. That alone, already brings about self-confidence, dynamism and strength in the child.

If the child has become acclimated, that is, if it has made the switch from school to family, then you could direct well-considered questions to your child, whether it would to like eat right away or first report about its lessons in school.

Phrase the question in such a way that the child senses that either one is fine with you, dear parents.

In this way, you train your child to openness, to security, to inner freedom and also to the ability and strength to make decisions.

If your child is in the first or second grade, then, in many cases, it's still appropriate to place on its chair or eating place its toy cat, teddy bear or doll – that is, its favorite stuffed animal or doll, with which the child first spoke in the morning.

When the child enters the parent's house after school and thus enters an accustomed atmosphere, it's possible that the little pupil of the first or second grade goes to the favorite animal or favorite doll, embraces it and tells the teddy or doll what its heart is full of.

It is also possible that when seeing its favorite toy, it remembers the morning conversation it had with the teddy, for instance. By remembering this, many a thing can become solved in the child: For example, thoughts of brooding and fear can be dissolved when seeing the teddy. Children forget easily. Through the teddy's presence, the dark clouds on the child's horizon pass by. Everything is okay now; the child is again playful and happy.

This small service of love by the parents, putting the cat, the doll or the teddy by the eating place, also results in the parents' learning important aspects from their child as time goes by. From what their child tells its favorite toy, they can perceive in time what difficulties their child is dealing with, in order to then carefully resolve them with it.

Stimulated by the favorite toy, by the teddy, the doll or the cat, abilities and talents in the soul and in the subconscious can break out, which are then recognized by the parents. They can then be encouraged by the parents or teachers. Such recognitions and help are particularly important for future years in life, perhaps for placement in a secondary school or for the choice of a profession, which should bring the young person joy.

In this way, and without great difficulties or problems, the child can mature into adolescence and adulthood. The child can learn to recognize itself and to have its own experiences, and to choose its occupation according to its abilities and talents – an occupation that the child likes and gives it joy.

The human being is forgetful. For this reason, dear parents, it would be good if you would record your child's behavior in its book of life. Also make notes about its reactions and answers right after coming home from school. All this gives information about the child's inner life and is of great importance for the future of the child.

Raising your child to think positively

Dear parents, strive to take your child seriously, so that it feels accepted and fully absorbed into the family.

Do not say to your child: "You don't understand this or that," when it wants to join in a conversation. Do not push it aside with the reasoning: "This is a conversation for adults; little Angie or little Max doesn't understand it." Through such remarks, you prepare the ground for an inferiority complex, which often becomes apparent only at a later time, when adults should be standing on their own two feet and proving themselves on a job.

Avoid having conversations in front of your child about your fellow people, conversations about colleagues at work, neighbors, relatives and acquaintances. Positive as well as negative conversations, particularly about close neighbors, strongly imprint themselves on the child's alert and active ability to react.

In later years, it then makes comparisons about other people; it thinks that as its parents described relatives, friends and acquaintances, so must those now be who are well, less well or even negatively disposed toward the now adolescent or adult person. People, who as children have heard much negativity about their fellow people, are negatively programmed by this.

Matter is permeated with negative forces. Every person calls up positive as well as negative forces, totally according to their programming and the luggage the person brought along from former lives. It's a big help for the person if the parents frequently give the child an understanding of the positive, that is, also showing it the positive that is in the people who are not well-disposed toward the parents and their children. Those who can do this create room for understanding, good will and tolerance in themselves, as well as in their children. The person becomes positive; the negative aspects that the soul brought with it from former lives gradually disappear unnoticed.

Negatively shaped people often become great pessimists who disparage everything that doesn't correspond to the thought patterns instilled in them and their schema.

Dear parents, that is an indication, which, if heeded, can spare the child much and help it, as well. And you, too, will view the negative with the eyes of an understanding, tolerant person who is in command of the situation.

When parents quarrel

If there is a quarrel among you, then do not carry out the conflict and altercations in front of your child or children. As already revealed, the ability of your children to register things perceives the finest nuances of the arguments. The child then no longer feels at home and that it belongs. It feels insecure and doesn't know which parent it should consider to be right, because the child loves both parents. It can go so far that, in the end, the child no longer knows which parent to go to, when it has questions or doesn't know what it should do when it feels drawn toward its parents and wants to cuddle, in order to feel the warmth and security of a happy home, the secureness that the child needs so much.

There is still a strong sense of justice in the little ones. They don't want to favor one parent or to treat the other one less favorably. The result is that the child withdraws into itself and becomes stubborn.

Depending on their soul burdens, children who lack the feeling of a warm and secure home become either stubborn or anxious or they sulk in every situation that reminds them of the atmosphere at home. Further consequences can be aggression, because the child feels rejected.

Dear parents, if there is some distance between you, no matter what the cause may be, then explain things to your child; however, do not do this without including what is positive and hopeful.

Do not cause your child to worry that perhaps things will not go well again between you.

Particularly between the sixth and twelfth year of age, parental difficulties can cause very great inner resistance in a child. When children live in such an atmosphere, then, in later years, they may rebel against their parents, society and against all people who think and live in a similar way as their parents.

I repeat, as it is very important for young people growing up:

When your child experiences your disputes or even merely a part of them, then explain to it what your argument is about; explain why there were altercations.

Thereby, it is important to emphasize the positive; for the positive can also become effective and clarifying for the parents in every quarrel, as long as they are of good will. If the parents now tell their child the mistakes made in the argument and their recognition from this for a further path through life together, then the child feels accepted, and despite everything, feels warmth and security and the parents' love.

When a child in this world is included in everything that goes on in the family, this brings about stability in the child and a feeling of belonging. Then it can become a stable and free person and also encounter fellow people openly and freely.

Free, dynamic people can approach their neighbor in the right way; they can respond to them in conversation, because they are not preoccupied with themselves and do not have an inferiority complex. This is why they can also concentrate accordingly. These are then happy people. Happy, free, positively attuned people are often ingenious thinkers, because their spiritual consciousness as well as their conscious mind and subconscious aren't stuffed full with nonessential and egocentric thoughts and wishes.

Dear parents, please recognize your responsibility to all your children. Do not be indifferent here.

What you fail to do with your child, because you do not want to practice restraint and only your own life is important to you, and perhaps because you treat your child merely as an appendage – for this, you will have to face responsibility according to the law of sowing and reaping.

The man who procreated the child, as well as the woman who carried it under her heart, are, from the first hour in which they both know that an embryo is growing in the mother's body, responsible for the embryo's life as well as for the child's life after its birth.

Dear parents, the material shell of your child is a part of you. The indwelling spirit body is created and given by God. Help your child as much as you can according to your capabilities, so that it become a diligent person, but don't overtax your child. Parents who actualize the divine laws feel precisely what the child needs as help and have the corresponding words to accompany it in the various situations of its life.

Dear parents, also help your child with its schoolwork, especially in the first years of school.

Favorite animal and favorite doll

When a child is doing its homework, then not only should a parent be present, but also the child's favorite animal or doll. The animal or doll, to which the child already told a lot in the morning, reminds the child of many a statement that can be important while doing its homework.

As I already mentioned, the child creates an aura, an energy cocoon, around the favorite animal or doll. It consists of thoughts of love, desires and longings, of thoughts of hope and confidence; good ideas also help form the energy cocoon. However, there are also thoughts and words of worry, of fear and despair in the cocoon.

These energies that were thought or expressed revolve around the doll, the favorite stuffed animal or another object, which the child loves. Through this, the doll, the animal or the object comes alive for the child, because it unconsciously communicates with the energies that it had emitted. Thus, the teddy bear or the doll is alive for the child. If similar feelings or thoughts come up in the child as in the morning or after school, when at home the child was allowed to put the teddy or doll on its chair, then these feelings and thoughts that come up begin to communicate with the energy field – the doll's aura or cocoon. This stimulates the activity of the consciousness. It is possible that the child again talks to the teddy or doll or tells its thoughts to the parent who is present while the child does its homework.

From this, the parents can then see what thoughts are preoccupying the child and can then perhaps recognize emerging difficulties in time and take remedial action.

In these encounters and communication with the favorite animal or doll, the child opens up. This makes it possible to gain deep insight into its inner life.

An alert, loving observer recognizes the inner processes in the child, its joy and suffering, its worries and hardships. However, likewise latent abilities and talents become rec-

ognizable. They can then be awakened more and more, encouraged and expanded upon in the corresponding schools or learning institutions.

It is advisable to write down the child's significant reactions in its book of life. Indispositions and illnesses should also be recorded in the child's book of life.

This book will become a valuable reference book; later it will help the adult person to gain clarity about some of the behavior patterns, which may first appear in adulthood.

Dear young person growing up, you have heard that the one who is not clouded, that is, surrounded by unimportant, unloving thoughts can be helped by their guardian angel – also when dealing with homework. The heavenly Father wants you to become a competent person. He wants you to combine the spiritual qualities, abilities and talents with the earthly ones, in order to contribute to the well-being of many people.

Before you start your homework, concentrate to within, where the Spirit of our Father is active, and pray. You have heard that every person is the temple – or the house – of the Holy Spirit. Ask God, our Father, to help and support you. Ask Him that via your guardian angel, He grant you help in coping with your homework. Therefore, ask for concentration and cheerfulness. Anyone with a cheerful heart learns more easily.

Surely your teddy, cat or doll also has something to say or you have something to tell them.

What do they have to say to you?

What do you want to tell them?

Has everything been said?

And what about what may be close to your heart, and you want to tell your father or your mother?

If you have not yet opened your heart, then do it now!

Through this, you will become free within and can concentrate better on your homework.

Now, with the help of your mother or father and with your teddy, cat or doll, you do your homework.

You also receive help from your heavenly Father and your guardian angel.

Once your homework is done, you have the hours afterward available to you.

Surely you have already thought about how you will spend the rest of the day, with schoolmates, with friends or alone.

When I say "alone," then I mean you as a person in the visible world. You do know from the book "I Tell a Story – Will You Listen?" that a person is never alone.

When a person is loving and friendly and lives with all fellow people in peace and friendship, then they also radiate profound peace. The one who radiates profound peace also radiates selfless love. Selfless love and deep peace, which emanate from a person, attract, in turn, powers of love and peace and light-filled, invisible beings and people, who also love selflessly and have profound peace.

Peaceful, selflessly loving children attract nature beings, for instance. We do not want to forget these little nature helpers, the nature and elemental beings. People call them imps, dwarfs, gnomes, elves, fairies and mermaids. You, dear child, like all good people, are surrounded by them.

If you would like to hear about them, then, I, Liobani, will tell you through your sister, Gabriele, what they do and why they live and are active in nature, in the air and water and why they are also among the children and adults who have light-filled and bright thoughts, who love selflessly and radiate peace, who rejoice and laugh. The nature beings are also happy when children hop and play, when they move about, play ring-around-the-rosy or other fun, harmonious games.

The nature beings like to play with the children who keep peace. They also speak to them. Can you hear them?

If not, then I will tell you about them.

A Narrative by Liobani

The invisible helpers, the nature beings and elemental spirits – their path of evolution, their appearance and activity

You have heard that every person has three spheres of consciousness: a spiritual consciousness – the consciousness of the soul – and the subconscious and consciousness, also called conscious mind, of the body.

All three spheres of consciousness are active. The state of consciousness of the individual person is according to the development of the spiritual consciousness.

Dear brothers and sisters, all forms of life are in constant evolution, in the divine worlds, in the pure Being, as well as in all of infinity and on the Earth, as well. This evolution means the development and unfoldment of the spiritual consciousness.

Everything that lives is consciousness, including stones, minerals, plants and animals.

All spiritual life forms developed out of one spiritual atom, which bears within itself the absolute, divine consciousness and thus, the whole of creation.

When a spiritual form starts to crystallize out of one spiritual atom, then, out of the all-encompassing consciousness, only the particle is manifested – that means, it becomes a form – that is designated for the lowest consciousness, that of a stone. Thus, the plain stones have the smallest consciousness bodies. They are a one-particle-consciousness.

In a powerful light-rhythm, the universal energy, God, brings the smallest one-particle-consciousness into evolution. The one-particle-consciousness is only one tiny spiritual particle. As a result of the irradiation of the primordial energy, this one spiritual particle develops into more and more spiritual particles until finally a complete spirit body of light has emerged: the spirit being.

A comparison:
It is similar to the egg cell in the body of a woman. If this ovum has been fertilized in the rhythm determined by nature, then a child starts to grow in the womb of the woman and mother.

Thus, the spiritual forms develop from one spiritual atom that becomes one particle – the child of this world, the human being, develops from one ovum.

All spirit bodies have a particle structure; one could compare them with small honeycombs.

The material forms, the human being, the earthly animals and plants consist of many, many cells.

Since in the Spirit, too, everything is evolution, that is, development, the spiritual consciousness also expands: the spiritual consciousness of the plain and simple stone becomes the mineral consciousness, the next higher form.

Stones, as well as the minerals, plants and animals, the nature beings and the spirit children are thus in evolution, in development.

The spiritual plant world develops out of the matured stone and mineral consciousness.

The animal world, out of the spiritual plant world.

And out of the matured spiritual animal forms, the nature beings.

Out of the matured nature beings, the spirit children. The spirit children become fully mature spirit beings.

The perfect spirit beings are matured, but continue to increase in light and power through continuous evolution.

Thus, the simple stone bears within itself a great development potential.

This is the evolution in the divine kingdom.

Just as with the embryo in the mother's womb, ever more cells develop, ever more spiritual particles emerge in the course of development. Out of these emerge the spirit forms, and in their matured forms, the spirit beings.

Now let us go back to the human being.

The human being develops from one ovum. More and more cells form from it, until it has become a human body.

Thus, you can see that the human body develops gradually, as do the spiritual forms.

I repeat: Once the stone consciousness has fully developed as a form in the spiritual realm, then this stone consciousness, the form, proceeds to the mineral consciousness. There it develops further. Then it goes on into the plant consciousness. The form of the mineral becomes a plant.

Within the plant consciousness – also called plant collective – the various types of plants are developed in the form of spiritual particles. In this way, energy assumes form and is then energy that has become form.

Therefore, the expansion of consciousness extends over all the different kinds of stones, minerals and plants, continuing through the animal species, up to the different kinds of nature beings. The nature beings also have different degrees of consciousness. For this reason, they also have different forms, each one looking like its state of consciousness. The consciousness of the nature being also continues to grow through the prescribed eternal rhythm of light.

Thus, among the nature beings, there are the so-called gnomes, the soil-goblins – also called the little soil-man – the forest beings – which human children call forest imps – and the elves, which are the female principles.

You will now probably ask what principles are.

You see, dear child, in the divine kingdom there are not two genders as here on Earth. In the divine kingdom there are principles, the male principle, that is, the man and the female principle, the woman.

The genders exist with human beings because the physical body has to procreate a physical body, in turn, for the incarnating soul, that is, a human being, in which the soul can incarnate.

In the divine kingdom, the spirit body is not procreated but develops from one spiritual atom, by way of stones, minerals, plants, animals, the spirit children and spirit beings.

Thus, you realize the difference: In the spiritual kingdom there are principles, among human beings, there are the genders.

Dear child, on Earth the spiritual is enveloped with matter and that is why spiritual caregivers are necessary, which primarily care for the spiritual substances, that is, the spiritual forms or rays, in the material forms.

That is why there are invisible plant and animal caregivers: the nature beings. In the cosmic event, every nature being works according to its state of consciousness.

These invisible helpers in nature are thus the nature beings. Since you come from the spiritual kingdom, you should know that the whole of creation – the purely spiritual creation that is invisible for you and the visible creation – is made up of three connecting powers. These connecting powers are also called communication powers. They are polarity, mentality and duality. In all forms – even in the simplest consciousness – the male or female principle is already indicated.

According to the spiritual, eternal, cosmic laws, like powers, like consciousness vibrations, attract one another.

If, for example, two beings or people are very similar in their consciousness, then they have the same or similar characteristics, predispositions and goals.

These corresponding characteristics, predispositions and goals are energies. Every energy communicates with the same or similarly vibrating energy.

In the divine kingdom, the common characteristics and predispositions bring about the unison of powers, that is, harmony and accord.

The same is also possible among human beings when two or more people put their characteristics, talents and goals into selfless service and fulfill their work and activity together and joyfully.

Among the nature beings, too, the same or similarly vibrating powers come together, that is, nature beings with the same or similarly developed consciousness.

Male and female nature beings, that is, dwarves and elves, also unite. They form a mentality vibration and work in the great cosmic event.

The respective state of consciousness of the spiritual life that is in evolution shows itself in its spiritual form. Stones and minerals, as well as plants and animals show their state of consciousness in their form.

The spiritually wise person recognizes the spiritual state of consciousness even in the material life forms.

Even the nature beings that cannot be seen with the human eye – since they are spiritual bodies – show their state of consciousness in their form. These forms of nature can be called elemental spirits or nature beings. Here, I will not make any great difference between these forms of individual states of consciousness, because every spiritual element is contained in the other. As long as the consciousness forms have not yet reached the expression of a fully developed spirit being, they are development forms, which I will call either elemental spirits, elemental beings or nature beings.

The state of consciousness of the human beings is also evident in the material body, their light and shadowed sides.

People's way of thinking and acting thus has an effect in and on their human body. When you are a few years older, you will understand this better.

I will explain to you the spiritual and material events more comprehensively, that is, in more detail, when you are able to understanding them correctly.

The spiritual forms, for example, the nature beings, cannot burden themselves; that means they cannot shadow their spiritual body.

Nature beings usually work together. Therefore, the same or similar consciousness vibrations are active, for instance, in caring for the spiritual substances of stones and minerals or for the spiritual substances of animals, for the part-souls of animals.

The consciousness of gnomes is not as far developed as that of the nature beings, which are active, for example, as caregivers for nature and animals. That, however, has nothing to do with the shadows or burdens of the developing spirit body. As I have already explained to you, the invisible beings of nature cannot burden themselves, because they do not yet have the consciousness of a spirit being.

Only a spirit being can incarnate into a human body and burden itself.

Dear child, it is still somewhat difficult for you to comprehend this spiritual development, evolution. I will give you a comparison so that you may better understand.

When, for instance, the feelings of love in a man become active in a woman and both desire a child, then the child begins to grow under the heart of the mother.

A mature egg in the woman's body is fertilized by the man's love sensations. It is vivified. It begins to divide. And out of this, result ever more cells, which join together and gradually form the physical body for the soul.

If the time has come and the child is mature enough that it can be an independent physical body, then it is delivered from the mother.

You can also experience and observe this with animals: The animal child is not put in the lap of the feminine animal. First, the egg cell in the female animal body is touched by the so-called sperm, the male powers, and cell division is stimulated.

The vivified ovum, the egg cell, is a single-cell organism. It still has a cell consciousness. The fertilized egg cell begins to divide itself. The division of the cells continues over and over again, until the child in the mother's womb – or with the animal, in the womb of the animal mother – has matured enough that it can separate itself from the direct nourishment through the mother's womb and become an individual body.

The form and appearance of the child may still be small. But all body parts and functions are present in and on the body. The small human being or the small animal continues to develop and grows and receives its energy from food, from the air and sun.

You see, dear child, similar things happen in the spiritual kingdom, in the heavens. We call this spiritual growth evolution. Evolution means development.

The flowing power takes on form in the spiritual kingdom when predetermined spiritual atom types become active so that the first spiritual particle emerges, which has the form of a stone.

Out of this first spiritual particle, more and more spiritual particles develop and fit together into one spiritual form.

With God, our heavenly Father, that is, in the eternal light, the spiritual evolution, the growth, develops out of one spiritual particle. The first evolution process is the formation into a stone, then into minerals, then into plant species, then the animal species, then the nature beings, all the way to the spirit being. Evolution also takes place within a certain species.

Thus, at the beginning of its existence, the gnome is, for instance, a nature being. It takes care of the plant and animal species that are not yet developed so far, especially the animals that live deep down in the soil and see daylight only when a big excavating machine digs up the soil. The animals that live in the soil cannot live on top of the soil. And that's why they suffer great pain when they are brought to the surface. The gnomes, which resemble clods of soil in their appearance, help these animals of the soil. They support them with the energies that they draw from the cosmos. In a similar way as in spiritual healing, they transfer these energies to the animal forms, helping and serving them in this way.

The gnomes' talents and capabilities are to serve and help these animal forms, because with their developed consciousness, with their radiation, they are closest to these life forms in their vibration.

You have already heard that like attracts like or similar things. This spiritual law is true for the entire universe.

Although the consciousness of the gnome is already a few light-energies further developed than the consciousness of the plant and animal species, nevertheless, a similarity to the plant and animal world is present. Through this, they are still very closely connected to these forms of development. Since like attracts like, the gnomes serve all those life forms that are one or more light-powers below their state of development. The higher consciousness always serves the one that is just below it. Therefore, nature beings that serve higher developed plants and animals are already further developed. They, too, work with the cosmic powers, helping the enslaved nature and the animals that need help.

The invisible nature helpers also help, for example, the half-parched flowers on the roadside, because flowers also have a consciousness and feel.

Dear child, all of nature and animals also feel the good and less-good people. They feel their radiating energy.

Thus, every inconspicuous flower feels your radiation.

Your radiation is what you feel, think and speak.

Feelings, thoughts, words and actions are energies, therefore, radiating powers.

Just as light radiates – you can see this especially at night when a light is burning and spreads its light – it is similar with your body. Your body radiates your feelings and thoughts, also what you say and do.

Your radiation has many colors and each nuance indicates your world of feelings and thoughts.

Your words and actions, as well, all your movements, are radiation and color. That is, then, your radiating energy.

For example, if you want to break off a flower or pull it out and you go to this flower with this intention – that is, with your thoughts that radiate – then the flower's consciousness takes in your radiating thought. Therefore, the flower senses your intention.

Thereupon, it sends out fine vibrations that say: "Please don't torture me; I want to continue blossoming here in the flower bed or in the meadow or by the roadside until I wither. That is my life, just as you have your life."

Dear little brother or sister, do you want someone to come and cut off your foot or your hand? Do you want them to kill you? You say that it is your life and no person may intervene in your life. That is correct. The same thing applies, however, to the plant and animal kingdoms. No person may deliberately intervene in the plant or animal world. But human beings do this very often – without realizing that plants and animals also sense and feel them.

Our second neighbors are subordinate life forms.

Subordinate means they are not yet fully developed like the spirit beings.

Our second neighbors are the animals, plants and also the stones. Every life form feels, because the eternal Spirit, the flowing, primordial energy, flows through the respective form of consciousness. Thus, every stone feels, because it is part of the stone consciousness.

Consciousness forms are bundled energies. Every spiritual form is life and feels.

You yourself know feelings. You feel joy and pain, suffering, hardship, hope and confidence; you feel all this and much more.

Your second neighbors, the animals, plants and stones feel like you do.

When you, for example, deliberately tear out a flower or break it off, then you have prematurely cut it off from its life force. Killed by a person, it withers away painfully. It feels that it was not able to fully live its life as a flower because a person intervened in its life.

When you feel the urge to simply, consciously, break off or bend a flower, then remember that all life feels.

Realize: Do not do to others, what you do not want to have done to you.

When a flower or many flowers, also grass, bushes and trees, were and are mistreated by people, then their spirit body sends out subtle sensations for help.

I would like to explain to you briefly the word "mistreat."

When people mistreats something, then they do so consciously. They want to destroy.

If this is done unintentionally, that means, when a person walks through meadows or through the woods and here and there bends flowers and grasses or steps on animals, then this doesn't happen intentionally. The life forms sense this and their pain is transformed into understanding for the hiker.

You must know that the spiritual consciousness consists of fine currents of love. These are drawn together into one love-current, since each life form's makeup and effectiveness is different, according to the state of consciousness of the life form.

The fine spiritual streams, the help impulses, which emanate from the flowers, plants, blades of grass and bushes that have been deliberately broken off or torn out, turn to the responsible nature beings. The fine spiritual sensations of the suffering second neighbor ask for help.

You see, in the eternal divine law everything has its order.

Thus, the nature beings are divided into reserves according to their state of consciousness, their talents and capabilities. Reserves are predetermined large areas in which the nature beings help and ensure that the flower children, the plants, the grasses, the bushes and trees receive spiritual care.

Nature beings that are assigned to a specific area of nature register the fine calls for help from the second neighbor. They then come and help, for instance, the broken-off flower or the flower unlovingly left by the wayside.

Out of the spirit bodies of the nature beings, flow cosmic forces that support the life in the pulled-out or broken-off flower, for example, and slowly release it from the external body, from the material shell. These helping and healing streams are the love-currents of our heavenly Father. The second neighbors worship His Spirit.

The healing and helping forces, which flow via the nature beings, help the flower child that withered too early and release its life force.

The divine life forces are at work in every flower, plant, in every blade of grass, bush or tree, as well as in every animal.

Part-souls have incarnated in many animals, which already have a higher developed consciousness. That means that many spiritual particles are combined, which form a developing spiritual body.

The life of the second neighbor that is passing away regresses slowly – under the radiating hands of the nature spirits.

The life rays of the plants and stones and the animals that do not yet have a part-soul, go back into the Earth's soul, supported by the energies from the nature beings.

The animal's part-souls go back into the spiritual development spheres of the heavens, if they are attracted from there for the continuation of their development. If they are not yet mature enough for this, then they slip into another animal body on Earth, which corresponds to the vibration of the part-soul.

Life is a continuous rhythm according to the eternal law. The eternal law is also called rhythmic life.

Birth and death, the coming and going, proceed according to predetermined laws, according to the eternal rhythm. The nature kingdoms are also included in this rhythm.

If this rhythmic life is disturbed by the wrongdoing of a human being, because many people seldom have respect for the life of their fellow people, for their neighbors and their second neighbors – the plants and animals – help is necessary in many ways and means. That is why there are visible and invisible helpers. The invisible helpers are the guardian angels and the nature beings.

The visible helpers are those people who feel closely connected with God and nature, who are sensitive to people in need, as well as to plants and animals.

In many cases, people who love nature, who know nothing about these nature helpers, often work together with the nature spirits. I will tell you how this happens.

A nature friend walks over the fields or hikes through the woods. He looks at the flowers, the bushes and trees in a friendly way. He senses the life in them and he feels connected with them. Unnoticed, he senses the fine vibrations that are emitted by the flowers, bushes and trees, which envelop him and with this, want to tell him: "You are a good person; you understand us. You are one with us. We are glad that you are walking through the meadows, fields and woods."

The small flower, for example, sends out sensations, which express something like: "Your heavy body, your foot bends my stem; but I was able to help that a good person, linked with God and nature, can be lovingly accepted and supported by many plants and by the soil."

People who are good and who have a close relationship with God are lovingly accepted and supported by the flowers and grasses, even when their foot bends a small body of nature. It was their task to support. This is how the plants serve human beings.

They also serve the animals that bite them off and eat grasses, flowers and plants. Certain flower and plant species are there to sacrifice themselves to higher life forms, for example, the animals, which need the flowers, grasses and many types of plants in order to live.

Dear child, recognize that in this way, God's love sacrifices itself in the form of plants, of flowers and grasses, and also in small animals, which are either stepped on, crushed or eaten by larger animals.

The larger animals, for example, cows and horses, do not see these many small animals; they take them in with flowers and grasses – and yet, these smallest animals suffer just as little from this as do the plants. Why? Because they are foreseen for this, to subordinate and give themselves to the higher life forms, which now need grass, or in winter, hay.

The life forms of the plant kingdom also form a carpet for many people who wander through meadows and woods, usually without thinking that they are stepping on countless flowers, grasses, plants and animals.

During their time of maturing, all these life forms are there to gladly sacrifice themselves to a higher consciousness.

However, if a nature friend comes along who understands this and who is close to nature, then there is a very fine and delicate jubilation in these many life forms. They are happy to be able to serve a light-filled person striving toward God, who loves nature and the animals.

As I already described to you at the beginning, not every flower and plant species is just now, in this year or at this moment, destined to be sacrificed. And it is certainly not foreseen that a person deliberately breaks off a plant, a flower, grass or a bush and then even leaves it lying by the wayside or on the road, where tractors or cars drive over it and torture it even more.

What do the nature spirits do?

I have already explained to you that the nature spirits also help these broken-off flowers or those left by the wayside. They hold their little spiritual hands around these tortured life forms and breathe on them with their breath, with the life force that flows through them, so that, slowly and sheltered from the light, they can wilt. In this way, the life ray can withdraw easily.

The natural law then leads the ray of life to where new life is forming again, to other germinating plants or flowers.

Thus, innumerable nature beings are constantly at work to help and support the plants and animals.

When a nature friend walking through the woods finds a suffering animal that has been shot or tortured in another way by a violator of nature, a so-called poacher, then the nature beings helped so that t the suffering animal is found: The nature being, invisible to the person, makes itself somehow noticed by this nature friend. For example, the nature spirit asks the spirit of air to blow more strongly into the bush or shrubbery. The spirit of air helps and blows, so that the bush or the shrubbery, in which the suffering animal is lying, noticeably rustles.

The eyes of the nature friend then turn to the shrubbery where this rustling was heard. And lo and behold, the nature friend then sees the suffering animal lying under the shrubbery! The nature friend and the invisible nature beings help the suffering animal.

The nature being takes care of the small part-soul of the animal, by causing calming rays to flow into the soul and body. In addition, it also lays its spiritual hands, from which strength and love flow, on the animal.

The people who are closely linked with nature help the small animal in their way. Perhaps, they must take it home in order to care for its body. If the person takes the animal home to care for it, then the nature spirit goes with this person and the animal only to the border of the reserve where the nature being works and is active.

The power of love, the help of the elf or the dwarf stays, however, with the suffering animal that the nature friend is also helping. The powers of love are also healing powers which continue to work in the part-soul of the animal and in its body.

Dear little brother or sister, you just heard about the spirit of air. You should know that in nature, there are also the spirits of fire, air and water. They are also called elemental spirits.

The four nature helpers, the forces of fire, air, water and earth work together with the nature spirits as a cosmic unit for the life in nature.

The fire spirit strives to burn as little as possible in nature, this means that, for example, people recognize in time when a forest fire is about to break out.

If a fire breaks out despite all their efforts, then the fire spirits also save and help and comfort; or they call the nature spirits and these – again, together with the fire spirits – call people, who may be reachable via the vibrations of their sensations.

Dear child, you know that fire is hot. Perhaps you have already felt it yourself, when you brought your hands too close to a burning candle or put your hands on a hot stove.

You would be very afraid; you would cry and scream, if your clothes suddenly burned or if you are in the house and fire breaks out.

See, it is similar for many plants, for the bigger animals, for example, the deer, the foxes, hares and all the small and tiniest animals that live in the woods and in the fields. When there is a fire and they cannot escape the danger in time, they suffer great, great hardship.

The fire spirits that were not able to extinguish the fire, because circumstance did not allow it, to save, save and save and try, perhaps together with the nature spirits, to call people who will extinguish the fire and try to smother the still smoldering fire with sticks or to stamp it out with their feet.

If, for example, the fire and nature spirits were not able to prevent a fire, then they endeavor to lead nature friends who perhaps are underway, so that they see the fire or smell it. The fire spirits, for example, rush toward the nature friends, surround them and influence their senses very gently, for example, their sense of smell.

The nature friend suddenly senses the smell of fire: "It smells like fire. Where can it be burning?"

Then, the fire spirits act on the nature friend's eyes, on the organ of sight. The nature friend looks up and sees smoke.

The fire and nature spirits then continue to work on the person's senses, who hurries toward the source of fire to put it out.

See, dear child, in this and in similar ways, the elemental spirits work to help nature, to protect the animals and also to call people, so that they may recognize and eliminate many dangers in time.

As has already been revealed, the water spirits also belong to the elemental spirits. They, too, are nature helpers. They serve the life in the waters. They help the water animals and also the water plants, which are, among other things, sources of food for these animals.

You have already heard about the earth spirits, the nature beings.

There are also the spirits of air.

The elemental beings, the fire, water and air spirits, also the earth spirits, are, as I already explained to you, helpers of nature. You can also call these four the forces of nature; they are energies that have become form.

The fire, water and air spirits can dissolve themselves, in contrast to the life forms that consist of combined active particle forms, such as stones, minerals, plants, animals and the nature beings, the gnomes, dwarfs and elves which resemble the spirit beings.

The nature spirits, the elves and dwarfs, are the furthest developed nature forms on the path of evolution. They stand upright and are comparable in size to a human child toffour to six years of age, but their shape and their facial expression are still coarse and bizarre.

Their facial features and their shape are coarser than in a human child – simply closer to the plant and animal world.

Dear child, the nature beings, for example, the elves and dwarfs are, as I have revealed, the furthest developed. This development stage is the preliminary stage to becoming a spirit child. A matured nature being, an elf or a dwarf that has developed all the elemental levels within itself, will then be attracted by spiritual parents, by spirit beings, according to the law of the heavens. It will be assimilated, and through their rays of love, will be reshaped and elevated to their spirit child; it is then a child of our heavenly Father. I will explain to you later how this takes place.

Dear child, as you already know, everything has its order in God's great plan of creation.

All of creation is based on the seven basic powers of God: on His Order, His Will, His Wisdom, His Earnestness, His Patience, Love and Mercy. These seven basic powers are the law of infinity.

All pure, complete spirit beings and all development forms, like the fire, water, air and earth spirits, which are also called elemental or nature powers, live and work according to the eternally given laws of God.

Everything has its order. Therefore, the fire, water, earth and air spirits are assigned to reserves, that is, areas or sections that they take care of – all according to their state of consciousness, to their level of evolution. There,as far as it is possible for them and as the eternal law allows, they serve and protect life, the life in material bodies.

You may have asked yourself what these spirit forms, also called nature forms, look like, where and how they live. I want to try to describe this to you – insofar as it is possible with human words.

You have heard that everything is development, that is, evolution.

The spiritual forms of the heavens come forth from one ray of light of the eternal Father, out of one spiritual atom and first become a minute form, a crumb that has only one spiritual particle as substance.

Just as a child grows from a fertilized egg cell in the womb of the mother, it happens in a similar way in the divine kingdom, in the purely spiritual development planes of heaven.

There, a ray of the eternal Father is compressed to one spiritual particle into which the eternal light radiates again and again, vivifying it, so that more spiritual particles develop from it.

At first, a crumb-like form develops from one spiritual particle, which continues to develop and gradually grows into a stone.

The development then continues toward a light-filled mineral, then to plants, animals, nature beings – the elemental beings are a part of the nature beings – then to the spirit child and in the course of further development, to a perfect spirit being.

Therefore, you now know: Out of one spiritual particle, more and more spiritual particles develop through the rays of light, which constantly go out from the eternal

Father. They then shape the form and the consciousness of all that is predetermined in the wheel of life of development, of evolution.

I have already explained evolution to you. But it is good to repeat this powerful event of evolution once more. It will then be better imprinted on your consciousness. I will explain what has been revealed from another perspective, so that it is easier for you to understand:

Once the life form, the stone, is complete and this form has its spiritual particles, the stone consciousness, then the form stone continues to develop. The next life form, also called entity, is formed again and again out of the particles, out of the existing consciousness.

The stone consciousness, that is, the stone, becomes a higher form, a mineral.

Several evolutionary steps are necessary until the mineral consciousness is built up, until all the cosmic rays of the minerals are active in this life form. Out of the fully developed stone consciousness, develops a higher form, that of the minerals.

The further life forms are then the countless species of grasses, plants, trees and bushes; this means that these further life forms emerge from the fully developed consciousness of the minerals. A radiation form always builds on the already existing radiation form.

In its further progression, once the consciousness of the plant kingdom is fully developed, for example, once the former stone or mineral consciousness is now a mighty tree, which has gone through all life forms, such as grasses, plants, flowers and bushes, then this life form gradually passes into the next higher level, namely, into the lowest animal form. There, evolution continues to the fully matured life form of the part-soul of an animal, which now has the strength and bears the radiation to stand upright and gradually become a being, which, in its further development, is akin to a child.

The transition from mineral to plant, from plant to animal, from animal to elemental form, the nature form, takes place bit by bit.

It takes place step by step, once a fully matured plant form is raised to become an animal.

We could call the first phase of evolution from the plant to the next higher form a "plant animal," since it contains both: the still existing plant species, but also the form of the animal.

Something similar happens when fully matured animal forms become small entities. We use the general term nature beings to describe these small entities.

The first small entities are still animal beings. The small upright body, which is already standing on two feet, still has animal features and, at the same time, the rudiments toward a nature being that walks upright. It is similar to a spirit child in its further development, but in its appearance, it still reminds us of animals.

The first small, but very formless entities, which condense to become a form and can dissolve again into flowing energy, are the fire, air and water spirits. None of these spirit beings can be seen with the human eye.

The developing spirit bodies, the elemental beings, the nature beings like the gnomes, dwarfs and elves, and the fully matured beautiful spirit beings – just as you are in heaven – can be seen only with the spiritual eyes. And that, only by people who keep their souls light-filled and pure, or who make them perfect again by refining their thoughts and senses. Thus, only the spiritual eye, the eye of the soul, can behold these inner processes, the spiritual.

If the soul now transmits what it has seen in the spiritual into the three-dimensional world, people can portray the air, fire and water spirits only as beings of this three-dimensional world in which you, dear human brothers and sisters, live.

These forces that live in higher dimensions, that is, the spiritual forms, can be conceived by human beings in the three-dimensional world only as I have described them. I, Liobani, try to transmit the spiritual forms to our sister in such a way, that another sister can draw them as the three-dimensional world imagines them, so that you get an inkling of what these forms of life approximately look like.

The nature beings, as well, the simple gnomes and the higher developed elves and dwarfs, which are also called goblins or gnomes, have been seen by the soul of an enlightened person and with the help of another sister who paints well, they will then be transmitted into the world of the senses, into your present three-dimensional world.

However, the spiritual bodies of these beings don't look quite the way people portray them. People explain or draw them in a way that is conceivable for this world.

I, Liobani, too, will explain the divine, eternal homeland and the eternal laws to you, in such a way that you can understand them in this world, as you are able to conceive of them with your consciousness.

I will describe the forms of the fire, air and water spirits and also of the nature beings so that you can visualize them and slowly feel into the spiritual realms.

When you picture these life forms, or when they are drawn, you should know that these pictures are given only for your human power of imagination, for the life of the three-dimensional world. Surely your parents will explain to you what the three-dimensional world is.

The air, fire and water spirits, as well as the nature beings are far more wonderful and beautiful than you could possibly imagine.

So that you learn the terms and what the development levels are called, I will repeat.

Air, fire, water and earth spirits are called elemental beings or nature spirits.

The air, fire and water spirits, insofar as they assume form, are figures that resemble animals and nature beings. We could also describe them as being half animal and half nature being.

The nature beings, the earth being, are certainly not foreign to you. You have heard from your parents or grandparents that so-called dwarfs exist. People draw them or form figures of them. These figures and pictures that are meant to represent the spiritual forms are also two or three dimensional. The spiritual eye that beholds the spiritual beings transmits what has been seen into the material world of space. These reproductions then merely resemble the heavenly forms; nevertheless, they are images of reality. In reality, the beheld spiritual beings are far more beautiful, lovely and harmonious.

The air, fire and water spirits are, as you have now heard, half-entities. Their arms and hands, legs and feet are merely indicated. I would like to describe an elemental being to you in such a way that you can relate to it on Earth as a human being.

The air spirits

Imagine an air spirit with tangled and windblown hair, similar to when a storm blows into your long hair and blows it in all directions so that your hair is completely tousled. You can imagine another picture of the air spirit: It has, for example, very colorful, thin, fluffy hair. Its hair reminds us of fine feathers that shimmer in the sunlight in many colors. The head is, at first – as with every being developing toward a spirit form – much bigger than the merely indicated shape. So that you can better understand: The head of a developing being is larger than the still unformed, merely indicated, spiritual figure, that is, than the spirit body.

Why? Because starting from the head, the rest of the form, the body, is formed; for the powers flow into the head and gradually form the spirit body.

The face of an air spirit is, like the whole body, still unformed.

The entire body of an air spirit can be compared to a cloud formation.

The color of an air spirit is approximately the color of a cloud on which the sun shines. Although the body is flowing energy that is already becoming form, it is, however, not yet fully developed. That is why arms, hands, legs and feet can be seen only in outline form. I would like to again remind you of a cloud formation: It looks like the air spirit.

Dear child, look up at the clouds now and then, watch their forms and their movements, and you will again remember the air spirits. They are the helpers for the animals in the air.

The air spirits also work with the fire, water and earth spirits. They, too, are attendants in nature and in the animal kingdom.

We want to ask our sister, who can draw so beautifully, that she draw the air, fire, water and earth spirits. And our sister, who interprets my pure sensations into your language, into your words, will tell her how people can imagine such elemental beings.

Dear child, all elemental spirits are in absolute harmony with the flowing energies of nature, with fire, water, earth and with the air. The elemental forces work together very closely, because no element can exist without the other.

Fire cannot burn without air, and the Earth cannot live without fire (the sun), water and the air.

The elemental beings, the air, fire, water and earth spirits, are helpers of all life forms, of the animals in the air, on and in the water, and on and in the Earth; they are also attendants and helpers of all plant species.

Thus, our heavenly Father cares for all life forms in a wonderful way.

The more developed entities always serve the less developed forms. Those that are less developed, that are in evolution, accept this willingly, because they know that the next-higher evolution level serves the still lower-developing forms. The lower forms give, in turn, from what they receive, since everything in all of eternity is based on giving and receiving.

Giving and serving, that is selfless love.

From the principles of giving and receiving, grow the mentality, the polarity and duality, the deep love for one another.

Selfless service bears within itself selfless love, and selfless love again bears within serving others.

In this way, eternity is filled with life and strength.

Dear child, all elemental beings have several tasks. One task of the air spirit is, for instance, this one: When a big whirlwind begins to sweep across the land, then the air spirits become active. They send out fine vibrations, tones that are also melodies, to the nature spirits and also to the fire spirits, in order to warn the people who are underway or have started a fire.

Among other things, the fine signals of the air spirits have the effect that some animals seek shelter while others can be brought into safety by the earth spirits. They are animals that let themselves be addressed by the air and earth spirits and hear these fine signals.

At the same time, the air spirits warn the many birds to seek shelter. The wind, which is directed by the air spirit, guides or drives them to where they are somewhat protected from the storm.

The fine signals that move through the air are intuitively perceived by many animals. They hole up, either under big trees, in the bark of trees, in the underbrush, under large leaves, or even in the soil itself.

The air spirits also give signals to the water spirits when the danger of the oceans or lakes becoming turbulent arises.

The air, fire, water and earth spirits also warn people to return in time to their apartments and houses or other places of refuge.

You will now ask: In which way does an air spirit make itself noticeable to a person, in order to make the person aware of the looming danger?

It may increase a gust of wind, for example, that blows through a person's hair and tangles it up. The person is startled, looks up to the sky and wonders: Is a thunderstorm or storm coming? The person sees how dark clouds are gathering and says: "Ah, now I must hurry up to get home," and running, reaches safety just in time before the whirlwind sweeps through the streets, cities, villages and over the land and a severe thunderstorm begins.

Another example:

A person is in a thick forest. It is a hiker or a forest worker who sees only a little sky through the tops of the trees.

The forest dwarf cannot help with its fine vibrations, which want to warn the person, because the person is either preoccupied with themselves or totally involved with work. Therefore, the earth spirit that recognizes the impending danger calls the air spirit. The air spirit sends out fine, delicate vibrations, which are like melodies, to the air spirits and asks them to direct a gust of wind to a bush or a tree that is close to the hiker or the forest worker. Thereupon, the air spirit strengthens the gust that begins to strongly shake the bush or tree. People who are close to nature and to God register with their fine senses the fine vibrations of the invisible helpers. The hiker or the forest worker notices the movement of the bush or tree. The hiker or the forest worker leaves the thick forest to look at the sky and determine whether perhaps a thunderstorm or storm is about to begin. "Ah," the person thinks: "a thunderstorm is about to start." The hiker says: "I have to hurry and find a safe place." And the forest worker thinks: "I'll stop my work and drive home quickly or find shelter on the way."

Dear brothers and sisters, that is the way people and animals receive help.

The plants, flowers, bushes and trees are also protected by the invisible helpers, the nature spirits and the earth spirits, to the extent that is possible for them.

The earth spirits – which, from a spiritual point of view, personify the elemental power of the Earth, have assumed the care of the plants, flowers, bushes and trees on their reserve – also send out fine vibrations to the nature children, the plants that blossom and live on their reserve. They warn them particularly when danger threatens. Some flower species then close their blossoms or calyxes; others send out fine protective vibrations, that is, fine tones that hold back the storm as much as necessary, to keep it from sweeping across them with its full intensity and strength and sweep them away, or bend and break them off.

For example, if flowers are broken or even trees and bushes are uprooted, then it often means the end of its development as a tree or bush.

It is, however, also possible that due to the environmental polution caused by human beings that the plants, bushes and trees are weakened and no longer have the resistance to protect themselves. Such children of nature will then be broken off by the storm or even uprooted, all according to how strong the life force still is in them, or which sickness has struck them. In most cases, the sicknesses in the nature kingdom were and are caused by the wrong behavior of human beings.

Many people think only of themselves and hardly have any relationship with their neighbors and with their second neighbors, the plants and the animals, or no relationship at all. These people think wrongly and also act accordingly. Therefore, not only plants and animals have to suffer, but also people; for they create causes, since they think only of themselves and have no regard for their neighbor and their second neighbor.

Perhaps you now ask yourself why the guardian spirit doesn't warn the human being when in danger.

If a person cannot hear because the five senses are attuned solely to external noises, to the world and to their own ego or because they do not listen to their conscience, then the nature spirits, the attendants and helpers of nature, do try to warn the person. However, they are successful in this only when people are not too caught up in their own thoughts. If the people love only their self and do not know that other life forms can also feel and suffer, they will be hardhearted and egocentric. They think only of their self and thus, seldom perceives the fine vibrations of the guardian spirit or do not perceive them at all.

You must know that many people believe only what they can see; only that is real to them – and in their opinion, everything else that they cannot see with their physical eyes doesn't exist for them. Some people at least still respect the life of animals, because they know from their experience with pets that these also feel. But when it comes to the feeling and life of plants, many shake their heads and cannot understand that grasses, flowers, bushes and trees also feel. Even the stones have the capacity to feel. Such people are very dulled in their disposition, and are imprisoned in their own world of imagination. However, since God loves all His children, He has help come to His human children in many ways. He helps through the guardian angel; He helps through good people and through the elemental beings, the nature beings.

Therefore, it is important that the human beings refine their senses and align them with infinity, as well as with the manifold life of animals, plants and minerals.

If people refine their senses through a good life and acknowledging and loving all life forms as animated powers, then they will recognize where danger threatens or who is well or ill-disposed toward them.

Those who make an effort in this way to love all people, animals, plants and stones maintain friendship with all the nature kingdoms and the elemental beings. Intuitively, they will have contact with their guardian spirit and with the pure, divine world.

Thus, those who acknowledge and love infinity, the invisible life, as a part of their true life will be served by the elements fire, water, earth and air in all the kingdoms of nature.

The fire spirits

Dear child, I, Liobani, will describe the elemental spirits to you in your language, so that you can understand me, I, who speak the language of light. I want to make an effort, again and again, to express with human words what lives and works in the invisible world.

While I explain, pictures and ideas will come up in you. If I now ask you: "What do you think a fire spirit could look like?" then already pictures come up in you.

Know that seen with the spiritual eyes, the fire, water and air spirits are not yet fully formed entities. Their energy body can dissolve in flowing air as well as in flaming fire or in the rays of the sun. The same applies to the water spirits; they, too, can dissolve in flowing water. As you already know, the elemental spirits are part of the evolution process. They are spiritual elemental powers. In the divine realms, they are called the four powers of development, and in the world, they are called fire, water, earth and air.

Like all elemental spirits, the fire spirit has a very big head when compared to its torso.

As you already heard, the elemental spirits' bodies of fire, water and air do not have a solid form yet. This means that their arms, hands, legs and feet, even the whole torso, are not yet fully formed as in a perfect spiritual body.

The fire spirit radiates the elemental power of fire. Imagine the fire spirit as being red. Think of a blazing fire that moves vigorously in the wind as the flames shoot up ever higher. Every now and then, the darting flames look like not yet perfectly formed shapes.

This is how you can imagine the fire spirit.

You can also discover the fire spirit in the flame of a burning candle.

Can you perhaps recognize a small figure in every flickering flame – a little fire spirit?

Dear child, ask your mother or your father to read to you these truths about the eternal evolution process and about the help that elemental spirits give, and to talk with you about this. And ask them to light a candle and to blow at the flame together with you. Perhaps your mother or your father will also see a little fire spirit.

And if you make your eyes very, very small, pulling your cheeks up high and looking through the slits of your eyes: the color of the flames and their radiation will convey yet another picture to you.

A fire spirit can also show itself in other colors and forms. From your point of view, the fire spirit can look very dark; this happens when it moves through a cloud of smoke.

We could say that although the primary color remains red, the fire spirit changes its colors and forms all accord-

ing to its activity, to where it is presently at work for the living beings that are entrusted to it.

So that you can have an easily remembered picture, I will ask our sister who can paint well that she paint two or three fire spirits: one in the primary color, red, another in the radiant bright light that is like the light of a candle and another dark fire spirit that is moving through smoke.

Both of us, you and I, Liobani, thank our sister who has painted two or three or even more fire spirits.

The guardian angels and nature beings work together

Many animals of the fields and woods become sick because of humankind's wrongdoing. They, too, get infections and are struck down by fever. A good forester is not always on the scene to help. Then the nature spirits endeavor to help. This takes place as follows:

The earth spirits ask the fire spirit to intensify the rays of the sun and hold open their hands. The fire spirit, which has been summoned, then intensifies the forces of the sun and radiates them into the hands of the nature beings. The forces of the sun and of the planets then light up in the little hands. The earth spirits lovingly transmit these powers, which are also healing powers, to the sick animal. The elemental beings help and heal in this way.

If there is danger that a fire may start in a house or in the woods, then the elemental spirits again work together. It is imperative to save life.

The guardian spirit of a person who is at the scene of danger calls to the elemental spirits; it is possible that it has little contact with the person it is protecting because the person directs the senses to other things and also does not live in accord with the harmonious powers of nature. The elemental beings receive the guardian spirit's fine waves of sensation and begin their effort to help.

The air spirit, for example, causes a noise in someone's room who may be able to help others. The person hears the noise, looks around and thinks that a window is open and that a draft has caused the noise. He gets up and goes to the window but sees that it is closed! He thinks: "There must be another window open or perhaps the one that was just checked was not closed well." The noise still resounds in the person's ears and he opens another door to see if perhaps a window in another room is open. "Ah," he thinks, "it smells like something is burning." He goes to the room in which his grandchild, Lisa, is doing her homework, and sees that she has lit a candle.

What is Lisa doing? She is playing with fire. She is holding a piece of paper to the flame.

Grandfather says: "Lisa, what are you doing there? You are playing with fire! Please, stop that! You put yourself and everyone in the house in danger!"

Dear child, what actually happened?

The fire spirit called the air spirit. The air spirit blew a strong wind through the windows of the room where the grandfather was, who should be warned. The brief draft that the air spirit blew through several cracks attracted the grandfather's attention, so that he went to see where the air was coming from.

At the same time, though, the air spirit in the other room in which Lisa was playing caused the air to circulate more intensely, so that the flame grew bigger. The fire spirit then increased the smoke of the burning paper. Then the air spirit blew the air through the door so that the grandfather could smell the smoke. Grandfather's sense of smell perceived the smell of fire. In this way, the danger was recognized in time and eliminated! The elemental spirits' help action was successful.

But things can also go differently. If people cannot be warned, because they cannot be influenced or guided by their guardian spirit and the elemental spirits, then a small fire breaks out that can turn into a huge conflagration.

Just like at home, the same thing can happen in the fields or in the woods. The tasks of the nature spirits are quite varied.

When a forest fire, for instance, has broken out, then the elemental spirits again work very closely together.

The air and fire spirits regulate the gusts of wind in such a way that the animals scent the danger with their fine instinct and look for another place where they will be safe.

The animals of the air are also warned by the fire and air spirits. However, fewer and fewer animals are able to perceive the fine warning calls of the invisible helpers, because their instinct is often no longer able to register these calls.

You might ask why fewer and fewer animals are able to be guided by the elemental beings.

This is because their power of perception, their instinct, has been reduced more and more and even largely stunted as a result of the environmental influences.

When animals have spent a long time in cities or villages, they absorb the vibrations of the aura of people and their communities. Through this, their natural instinct is changed. The animals' power of perception is also reduced by the disharmonious noises coming from machines, engines and aircrafts. Their instinct is then stunted or is oriented to human beings and their atmosphere, in which the animals live. And animals that live with people have lost a lot of their fine instinct.

The pollution of the air, of the earth and of the waters also has an effect on the animals' fine sense of perception. Because of this, not every animal is able to perceive the fine warning calls of the elemental spirits. That is why the animals often have to endure great pain.

However, they are not left to their fate. The earth spirits help the best they can. They soothe and heal with their light-filled hands, with which they absorb the healing rays of the sun and of the planets. When necessary, the fire and air spirits will also do what they can to help.

Working together with all other elemental spirits and the guardian angels, the earth spirits also strive to help and save people, animals and plants that are in need. In some cases, they help and guide people via their own thoughts: Suddenly a person has the idea that they should go to this or that place. This thought impels them and they do it.

Later, they find out that an accident took place where they had been before, which they were able to escape thanks to this thought input.

People who have a lot of love for animals and plants, indeed, for all of nature, can be guided much more easily by their guardian spirit and the elemental spirits. Then, all the detours are not necessary before the person grasps what it's all about. A sensitive person will be guided via their fine senses which, as you have already heard, are their antennae.

The more sensitive the senses, the person's antennae, the more they will register with the inner senses of the soul all the things of life that they cannot perceive with their earthly eyes, but which surround and guide them according to the eternal universal law. The fine senses can also be compared to magnets: They attract that to which they are attuned. Many people are guided in this or similar ways. They may not know why they suddenly go here or there, but the guardian spirit and the elemental spirits know.

You see, dear child, that is true help; that is the real, selfless collaboration of the positive forces.

The water spirits

Surely you wonder what the water spirits look like and what tasks they might have.

What happens, for example, when a fire has to be put out with water?

Here, the water spirits have to take care that the many living organisms in every drop of water don't have to die or suffer in the fire.

Long before a fire breaks out, the earth spirits recognize the danger and signal to the water spirits what can happen and that people will need water to extinguish the fire.

The water spirits – human beings also call them water fairies or water nymphs – will now alert the microorganisms on their reserves, from which the water is taken for putting out the fire. The fine sounds that are emitted by the water spirits are signals for these microorganisms. These microorganisms hear the fine signals of the water spirits in the innumerable water drops and protect themselves by withdrawing to those areas of the water reserves from which no water will be used for extinguishing the fire. At the same time, the water and earth spirits make contact with the Earth's soul. Among other things, the Earth's soul maintains those life forms that don't yet have a part-soul. The responsible area of the Earth's soul that supplies these microorganisms with cosmic energy, we also call this part the collective area, then withdraws the life energies from these microorganisms that live in the endangered zone and that don't perceive the water spirits' subtle warning calls. As a result of the elemental beings' help, there is hardly any life left in the water that is then used to put out the fire.

Dear brothers and sisters, everything I have described here with your words takes place in just a few moments in the spirit.

If, for some reason, there are still microorganisms living in the water used for putting out the fire, the fire spirits endeavor to help them as much as it is possible for them.

Similar things happen when water is boiled in a kitchen, in cafeterias, in restaurants or factories. Wherever water is heated or brought to a boil, the air, fire, water and earth spirits are at work, to serve the higher and lower life forms.

Generally speaking, it would be better for humankind if they would not pollute this beneficial water so that it would not have be treated or boiled. If the water were heated only slowly and not brought to a boil, then the microorganisms would remain in the water drops and would not have to die.

For the microorganisms in water drops are also humankind's helpers, that is, they are health-giving for the blood and intestines. If water is merely heated and not boiled, these microorganisms stay alive, to a great extent.

The fire spirits also serve the microorganisms that suffer because their minute bodies are injured by boiling water or a firestorm. The fire spirits increase, for instance, the rays of the sun that fall on the suffering animals. In this way, they ensure that these tiny organisms receive relief from their suffering or receive healing.

The elemental spirits are also little midwives. For example, they help a dying animal so that the life-ray can withdraw more quickly into the Earth's soul, the sustainer of this life-ray, which absorbs it once more, that is, draws it in.

Dear child, when you hear this, you will certainly ask: Why doesn't the life-ray withdraw without the help of an elemental being?

The tiny bodies of the microorganisms tense up their bodies out of fear. The life-ray cannot withdraw due to this tension, and thus, it is kept back. The fire spirits now help the microorganisms to relax: They have a protecting and calming effect on them so that either the life-ray can withdraw into the Earth's soul, or the tiny animal can continue to live.

What do the water spirits look like?

Within its development sphere, every elemental being has several stages of development, which are also called development phases or development periods. The water spirits also give themselves different forms, according to their consciousness.

First of all, the water spirit can look very similar to a beautifully formed ocean wave, and its head resembles a mighty whitecap. Eyes, nose, mouth, arms, hands, legs and feet look like large water drops joined together, like smaller and greater amounts of water. The water drops can be compared to innumerable body cells. The water spirits' elemental form is made up of many water drops. Every water drop contains many microorganisms.

Yet other water spirits look different, according to the life in the water drops. The water spirits work solely in the water. Every now and then, the body and the head are similar to the earth spirit, but the arms, hands, legs and feet are still like fins, similar to water animals. This elemental form can also dissolve again in water, that is, it can transform itself. We will now ask our painter to paint how you can imagine a water spirit.

The water spirits which, as you have heard, are also called fairies and nymphs, care for and look after the various types of water animals and water plants. They understand the language of the fish; they know the sounds of the individual animal species and understand their language, because the world of sensations of the many fish and water plant species is active in them.

The pure spirit beings, the children of God, as well as the elemental beings, all glorify the Creator-God and serve selflessly. All of eternity is based on selfless service. All of them, the children of God and the elemental beings, serve according to their consciousness.

You have heard that the elemental beings have their reserves or areas in which they selflessly serve.

The more a life form approaches the matured nature beings, meaning, the filiation with God, that is, developing toward a perfect child, the more encompassing will be its activity in all of creation. Once a nature being has been raised to be a spirit child – because it has developed and activated all seven basic powers of the Father – it can move in all of infinity. Therefore, this means that the spirit beings are mature. They are no longer on the path of evolution. That is why they are able to move in all of infinity with their consciousness.

This also applies to you, dear child! Once you cleanse your soul, then your eternal consciousness becomes clearer. You uncover it by exposing what envelops it. This has the effect that you are open for infinity and that some day, you will be able to move again as a pure being of the heavens in all of infinity. Then, all the planes of heaven and the many spiritual stars and suns are no longer foreign to you. You have again discovered them through a selfless life. And then, with your consciousness, you can be everywhere because you solely do the will of the Father.

The cosmic mobility and flexibility are thus inherent in those beings that have totally opened their consciousness and are the conscious children of God who have been received into the sonship and daughtership.

Our eternal Father bears within Himself the Father- and Mother principle. The eternal Father is Father and Mother at the same time.

I will explain these spiritual correlations more clearly to you later. But first, remember:

The elemental beings don't speak about the heavenly Father, because they are not yet children of infinity but are developing into full beings, which will be raised to filiation only once they have opened all the nature kingdoms and have been received into filiation by a dual pair, that is, by two spirit beings, a spiritual man and a spiritual woman.

You have already heard about the spiritual birth in the book "I Tell a Story – Will You Listen?"

The elemental beings, which mature to become full beings, speak of the Creator God, of the All-Spirit, who is also called the primordial Spirit. Whether you hear or read the words of the Creator God, All-Spirit, or primordial Spirit, you should always know that it is one Spirit, the omnipresent power of our heavenly Father who streams throughout infinity.

Our heavenly Father is a being, therefore, He has a spiritual form as do all other spirit beings. However, His radiation power is stronger than the power of all beings together.

I will now go back to the water spirits in my story and explanation.

Thus, the water spirits take care of the water animals and water plants. They can dive down into the deepest depths, where there is likewise life. There are animals and plants there that have completely different living conditions than the fish that swim in the upper levels of the lakes and oceans, or than the water plants that live just below or on the surface of the lake or ocean.

The water spirits are the jolliest among the elemental spirits. They like to celebrate small and larger festivities. They invite many big and smaller fishes to these. The water spirits rarely celebrate only among themselves; they often ask the air and fire spirits to join in their celebrations.

The festivities take place especially when a continent turns away from the sun; you call it sunset. Then the water spirits announce the celebration of harmony. During the celebrations in the evening, the light-fish – there really are such fish – are the lanterns. The small and larger fish play rare games and perform beautiful water dances.

When a continent turns away from the sun, when the sun goes down, then it sends red rays across lakes and oceans. This creates a beautiful color symphony and harmony and a very special beautiful tone; for an air spirit very delicately ruffles the surface of the water so that small waves develop. It is the air spirit "Mild Wind," one name among many, that prepares the celebration and keeps the water in motion, so that the water moves especially beautifully where the celebration takes place, ruffling and producing small waves. A fire spirit, whose name is, for example, "Light Shimmer," that is the name of one of many, glides on the red ray of the sun over the ruffled

water that the air spirit Mild Wind is keeping in motion. Songs out of the depth of the lakes and oceans rise up to the water surface. It is the fairies and nymphs who adorn themselves with beautiful water plants for the celebration and slowly rise up in song. After the preparations for the celebration, more air and fire spirits arrive. The singing fairies and nymphs that rise from the depths of the lakes and oceans extend their hands to the air and fire spirits and dance a round dance with them to honor the Creator-God.

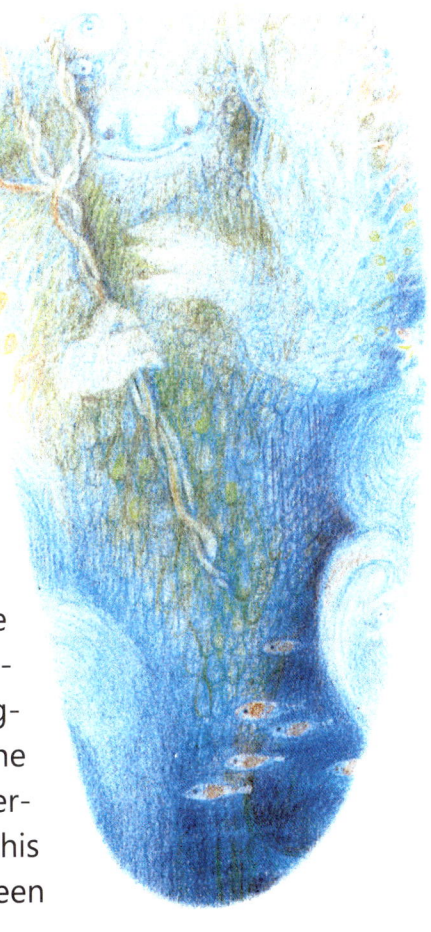

The air, fire and water spirits move on the ruffled waves, to praise the life, the Creator-God in all Being.

The many small and bigger fish hop and play games, a kind of ring-a-round-the-rosy, and dance around the harmoniously moving elemental spirits.

Suddenly, away from those who are dancing, the ocean moves. With great pageantry and might, one of the kings of the oceans, merman, rises up. He raises his trident, a reed that has been bent in such a way that it has three points. It is entwined with water lilies. He says: "My friends, you dancing elemental beings and you hopping fish, you are too loud!"

You must know that the elemental forms are all developed to a different degree. This results from the corresponding vibration degrees of the atoms in the air, as well as in the fire and in the water. Thus, for example, the form of the merman is more highly developed than the forms of the nymphs and the water fairies.

This means, for instance, that the water drops that make up the form of the merman contain more highly developed life forms of microorganisms.

But when he looks into the shining faces of the amazed elemental beings, merman "Prudence" realizes that he made a mistake.

What happened that a king of the oceans, the merman "Prudence", got upset and made a mistake?

During the dance of the elemental beings, the ocean ruffled up more strongly, because ever more air spirits moved the water and, at the same time, danced with the fairies and nymphs. This created a larger wave that rolled to the coast and crashed against the rock on which the merman Prudence had rested enjoying the evening sun, which irradiated and warmed his scale-like body.

However, when he saw the amazed fire and air spirits, his face became gentle and he himself began to turn in circles. The nymphs and fairies, the air and fire spirits danced around King Prudence, the merman. He felt flattered and raised his trident.

A lively air spirit swept into the trident, which splashed down onto the water, making even bigger waves.

The king of the oceans, the merman, raised his trident again and called: "Hear, hear, the frog king is announcing himself."

From far away, a melody could be heard by the singing and dancing elemental beings. It was the voices of the frog king "Harmony Hop" and his wife "Fine Symphony" and the many frog children and brothers and sisters, who all joined the elemental beings in their song and dance. It was a great orchestra of nature which could be heard far into the All, the universe.

And the person who loves nature and all beings hears the glorious melodies of the elemental beings and of all the children of creation and nature that praise and honor God, the Creator.

The day draws to a close; evening spreads and the light of the sun slowly fades. But nature's orchestra rises to a crescendo; the elemental beings, the fish and the frogs let their full melodies resound in thanks to the eternal Spirit who is also their life.

This part of the Earth has turned away from the sun completely; you would say the sun has set.

The fire spirits slowly withdraw into the atmosphere; they rest on a light-filled cloud or on a warm stream of the sun's energy until they welcome the new day again. Nevertheless, they are ready at all times, if their help is needed during the night.

The air spirits set the wind in motion once again and then withdraw to where there are very light breezes. This causes the ocean to move more quickly, the billows and the waves become larger. The fire, air, water and earth spirits rest in the cycle of day and night, but all of them are always alert, ready to help and serve, if there is need.

The celebration is over.

King Prudence, the merman, turns to the fairies and the nymphs and asks them to accompany him to the depths of the sea, to his great water palace.

Only the frogs continue to croak and sing their song in honor of the Creator-God who created them.

The water palace, deep below the surface of the sea, certainly looks peculiar, but is very beautiful. It is entwined with many rare water plants that are found only in the depths of the sea.

Dear little brother, or sister. I would like to describe the water palace of the merman Prudence and his wife.

Two beautifully formed boulders touch one another with their points. There is alarge space underneath. Wonderful and rare water plants grow above both boulders that seem to blend into one another. They also grow into the water palace, into the great inner room.

In this large room there are rare stones that are covered with a blanket of plants, similar to stones covered with moss. These are the chairs or small benches for the water family.

The merman invited the fairies and nymphs into his palace. There, they met his wife "Lovely Pearl" and the children, "Little Hop," "Soft Moss," "Lovely Tender," just to name a few of the children of the king and his wife "Lovely Pearl."

The merman's family, his wife and children, wear larger and smaller crowns, according to their spiritual development and the consciousness of the animal species, which are in the water drops that go to make up their water form.

The merman Prudence sits on his throne of stone and his wife gives him his crown, which is of woven water plants. Beautiful shining sea shells are worked into the crown.

His wife, Lovely Pearl, also puts on her crown and greets the fairies and the nymphs.

The merman's family wants to honor their friends, of course. And so, the children are asked to bring the fairies and the nymphs small garlands and crown-like objects and to put them on their heads. The young fairies and nymphs receive garlands, and the older ones, crowns.

The "children" of the merman's family are also formations of water that have linked with the higher energy power that has taken on form. This means that in the forms of the "children," which are also able to dissolve, there are tiny organisms with a lesser consciousness than those in the water forms of the "parents."

Two of the decorated fairies take some vines that are hanging down from the rocks into the room and play water songs on them as if on a harp. The elemental spirits that are present dance and move harmoniously to the water melodies.

The first dance, of course, is dedicated to the merman Prudence and his wife, Lovely Pearl. They open the dance and all those who want to dance do so to express the harmony that is inherent in them.

Midnight has passed and soon this part of the Earth will receive the first rays of the sun again.

The fairies and nymphs say goodbye and return to their water reserves to rest until the new day wakes them with the sun's rays, so that they may fulfill their services as elemental spirits.

You will surely wonder whether the big oceans and large lakes

have only one merman, whether there is only one king of the oceans?

Oh no, the higher developed water spirit is called Neptune by humankind.

So that you may better understand, I took the terms that people have chosen for the higher developed water spirits: "merman and merwoman," for on every level of development there are the male and female principles. The merman, as we want to call him, has various reserves under him. He glides through the various reserves in order watch over the life forms there and also to help when necessary.

Several smaller lakes together are under the responsibility of one merman. The very large lakes have their own merman, a king of the lake.

The life in the smaller lakes is cared for by the nymphs and water fairies, in whose water shapes live microorganisms that are already more highly developed. But a merman is also responsible for these small lakes. The spiritual radiation of the microorganisms makes up the respective consciousness of the forms of the water spirits.

Home and School

Closing the day in the family

The true stories that your mother, father, grandparents or one of your older brothers or sisters have read to you, surely let you realize that harmony and consonance of forces exist in all of infinity.

You should also strive to maintain harmony and consonance of forces within yourself and then at school with your schoolmates, in the family, with your parents and brothers and sisters.

In the rhythm of day and night, the powers of the universe, the All, have a different effect on the soul and person, depending on the soul's burden. The light of the day affects soul and body so that the person will recognize that part of their burdens that the day activates in them, as well as their degree of maturity. The night's radiation serves mainly for the soul's recovery. While the body sleeps deeply, it causes the soul to go to those spheres that it has opened, that is to say, that have opened to it through actualization. Thereby, the light-filled soul experiences the freedom and the awareness that it is a being of the All.

Dear child, for you, too, the day draws to a close.

In the evening, family members come together to close the day and to share the evening hours in a familial atmosphere. If everyone wants to have harmony in their family, then each one should strive to be open and honest. An open conversation about what needs to be done or about what moves each member of the family leads to mutual trust.

You, too, dear child, should participate and express what made you joyful or what you are sad about and think about. If you still feel very attached to your favorite animals or to your doll, then you should bring them along to the family talk.

To assure that harmony and the consonance of forces are maintained in the family, what went on during the day should be talked about every evening, a kind of review should take place. If you like your teddy or your doll or cat very much, then they could also say something.

As a reminder for the parents: Whatever the child says to the teddy, the cat or doll is the life of the thoughts of the child. A kind of aura or thought-field develops around its favorites. When the child then starts to think the same or something similar that clings to the favorite animal or doll, then this field of feelings, the energy that clings to its favorites, starts to vibrate more intensely and emits small thought-beings, that is, thought-energies. These then remind the child, for example: "That's how you thought," or "that's how you still think," or "because of your thoughts, this or that gave you joy or brought you difficulties."

The thought-forces around the teddy, doll or cat can bring a lot into movement in the child that would otherwise have become fixed in the subconscious and later flowed into the soul.

In this way, the child can be spared many difficulties. It learns to think clearly and attains a confident attitude toward human mistakes and weaknesses; it learns to be above the human aspects.

A doll, cat, or teddy can be useful for the child in many ways. In many cases, these favorites are its best conversation partners. They have time and are patient, until the child learns to concentrate and to plan its day in a lawful way; until it has learned to be selfless, that is, to act impersonally.

The first step to an impersonal life is: Be impartial. Do not allow your fellow people to influence you to act against your conviction. Do not think badly about your neighbor, just because others do this, and do not act against your neighbor because others do this. Those who discipline themselves to become selfless will not boss their neighbor around or force their will on them.

A noteworthy sentence to become happy or to stay happy is: Become impartial, then your life will be impersonal.

Dear child, before you go to sleep after the family talk, do as the elemental beings do.

If you have any, listen to beautiful, harmonious music with your brothers and sisters. Perhaps your father or your mother will join you. Teddy, cat and doll are also invited, of course, and shouldn't be left out. The best would be to bring all three along, since they are patient listeners. Harmonious circle dances to harmonious music can also calm the body and prepare it for a healthy sleep. Quiet, harmonious songs likewise have an effect.

Harmonious sounds and movements or harmonious colors, forms and fragrances bring about a balanced body rhythm and a balanced vibration.

When, namely, the body sleeps quietly and harmoniously, it finds the necessary deep sleep during which the soul can move away from the body and enter higher, light-filled spheres where it draws strength and peace.

When the soul goes on its journey at night, then it is connected with the sleeping body by the so-called "silver cord." The "silver cord" could also be called the information cord or band; for as soon as the sleeping body goes into a lighter state of sleep or when danger threatens the sleeping body, then the traveling soul registers this via this silver cord.

The silver cord or information band is a fine, delicate vibration that connects soul and body. You should know that when you sleep deeply, your soul, your second body, can go far away into infinity, to more light-filled and shining planes, in order to come into contact with beings of light there. Your soul feels free there, for in your body it feels like it is imprisoned. When you sleep deeply, it may feel the freedom of infinity.

Think about this when you now go to the bathroom to prepare your body for the night and for sleep. Surely your mother will help you when you take a bath or a shower and brush your teeth.

An advice for the parents, especially for the mothers:

Water is a cleansing and neutralizing element. If possible, it would be good if your children would bathe or shower after the day that has brought them so many different things, joy, suffering and sorrow. I would also advise this for the whole family and for all who read this book.

During the course of the day, people attract harmonious as well as disharmonious vibrations. They cling not only to their clothes but also to their aura, the fluidity that surrounds the person. Even the fine body hairs are antennas that attract and hold many vibrations, which then radiate out again; for everything that a person feels, thinks, speaks and does is what people attract and what they radiate.

When negative vibrations are picked up, they don't necessarily have to be absorbed by the soul immediately, not even when the same or something similar is present in the soul. For the time being, the body serves as protection. At first, the harmonious as well as the disharmonious vibrations cling to the clothes, to the fine body hairs and also to the magnetic aura, the vibration field that surrounds every person invisibly. Only over the course of hours or days, will the magnetic soul absorb what has not been neutralized until then.

Misconduct cannot be washed away with water. However, vibrations that are picked up from furniture and the most varied objects can be neutralized with water. Problems and difficulties are also vibrations as well as everything that people say to their fellow people. If someone who has listened patiently to their neighbor's problems and difficulties thinks about them and moves the neighbor's problems and difficulties for too long, then it is possible that these vibrations enter their own subconscious and have an effect there, depending on what they thought. As long as the subconscious has not yet absorbed such vibrations, they can be neutralized in time by cleansing the body with water.

However, if negative vibrations cling to the aura for a longer period of time, they enter the subconscious. From there they radiate – according to their intensity – to the nerves, organs, glands, hormones, to the whole organism – depending on the vibration and on what the person, who was spoken to about these problems and difficulties, thought, spoke and did.

Water washes many things away and neutralizes them. That is why it is advisable to bathe or shower in the evening.

Clothes that were worn during the day should not hang in the bedroom; they also radiate whatever the day has brought. This radiation can affect the sleeping person. It would be good to hang the clothes by an open window in another room, or in the fresh air outside of the room. The air, the wind, the sun and moon particles also neutralize many vibrations.

Dear parents, try to give your children insight into your behavior and explain your thoughts and actions to them.

Please don't tell your children: "This is the way we want to do it and this is how you have to do it!"

Explanations stimulate understanding. The child receives the certainty that it is taken seriously by the parents and brothers and sisters, and thus feels like a member of the family.

Dear parents, do not have a determining effect on your child, but endeavor to guide your child and to take it seriously, for there is a lively and mature soul in the child. Give your child advice and recommend this and that. But do not dominate.

Avoid every didactic way of speaking. Not every child can take this; especially not the spiritually alert soul that senses freedom, and experiences this at night when the child is sleeping. This discrepancy between the freedom during the night when the soul moves in vast realms and the imprisonment during the day, when a person has a determining effect on its body and soul cannot be tolerated by every child.

If your child has problems, explain to it that especially prayer can solve many problems – and that a correct, trusting prayer is a dialog with God.

The tasks in a family should not become mere obligations, but everything should be done for the joy of doing it.

The child should always feel secure and understood in the family. That is why the day should be closed together; it would be good if parents and children would do this with a joint evening prayer. In order to go into deeper prayer, I advise you to quiet down with harmonious music beforehand and perhaps do harmonious body exercises. In this way, the body attains a higher vibration and the person gains distance from the daily thoughts and from everything that still preoccupies them. Whether the prayers are offered to the Eternal aloud or silently, should be left to each one.

Recognize the difference between obligation and a sense of obligation: An obligation can be loaded upon a citizen of the Earth, often, even forced upon them. A sense of obligation is the inner attitude and the inner strength to do what has to be done with inner joy and love and to be able to thank God in the awareness that the soul is not of this world.

There are plenty of obligations in this world. It is enough for the child that it has to go to school and that it has other daily obligations that are unavoidable or that the laws of this world demand, because the person is a citizen of this world.

Therefore, a person should be left their free will regarding a spiritual attitude toward life – this includes the small citizens of the Earth. However, that doesn't mean that everything that the little citizen, the school child, wishes and what it wants should be fulfilled. In many cases, a serious, yet loving tone of voice is sufficient. Consistency with understandable explanations brings much better results than strictness and harshness.

People of the spirit strive to bring the worldly laws into accord with the spiritual ones as much as possible. When this is not possible, then each one has to decide how they want to act. Everyone is given free will and everyone should think and act according to their state of consciousness.

I would like to again speak about prayer: Praying together would be very advisable and good, for it holds the family together.

If this joint prayer is not possible for whatever reason, then either the father or the mother should pray with the child.

Short prayers, prayers of thanks and petition come from the deeper layers. They could be considered heart prayers. On the other hand, long prayers are often merely reeled off, and have little effect.

Dear parents, place your child into the care and protection of our heavenly Father again and again.

God is the Spirit of our eternal Father, who lives in all of us.

And give your child into the care of its guardian angel.

And do not worry by being overly anxious. That doesn't mean that you should be careless. But you should not worry unnecessarily and out of worry, project with your words into your child something that may not be in it – for example, by creating insecurity or fear in the child with your own anxiety.

Be prepared to help and serve at all times, as the elemental beings do – also at night if the child needs help. That is truly being with and for one another; this is Christian life in practice.

Dear child, I wish you a blessed night – as do your parents and your brothers and sisters.

The Spirit of our heavenly Father watches over all people, souls and beings. And the guardian angel accompanies the soul when it leaves the sleeping body and goes to more light-filled spheres, where it feels freedom.

Know that you are secure. Good night!

The morning

The morning dawns. The family awakens. Grateful to God, they welcome the day. Either the father or the mother awakens the school child calmly and lovingly, if it is not yet awake on its own. Until the children are about nine or ten years of age and beyond that, they are still very much oriented to their parents, to their vibrations, that is, to what they respectively radiate.

The little ones long for love and secureness and are often terribly upset and troubled when their father and their mother speak in a different way than what they feel; for they intuitively sense how and what parents think and in what frame of mind they are.

Especially mother and child are encompassed by a very tight invisible band. This comes especially from the child, who still feels comfortable at the mother's breast. She was the provider during the first days, weeks and months of life, at whose breast the child lay and from whom it received.

Many vibrations from the nursing mother are transmitted with the mother's milk to the child. All of her sensations and thoughts imprint the substance of the mother's milk. They can be transmitted to the child if the same or similar vibrations are in its soul. Also, the attitude and the love of the father for the mother, of the husband for his wife, are of essential significance for the child. Similar to the infant and the growing child, which develops more on the mother's vibration – or comes under the influence of her worry, fear and hardship – the mother, the woman, has become a part of the man, of the father, whose vibrations she absorbs, moves in herself and again radiates. The mother transmits to the child a part of her daily vibration with the mother's milk. Thus, in many cases, the child is shaped by the mother's vibration – all according to the maturity of its soul.

For the parents' further understanding:

Through the sperm, which is the life and bears the man's basic nature and characteristics, which gradually affect the woman's genes, she becomes a part of the man, if the shadows or the light-filled sides of her soul do not have a stronger effect.

If the parents love one another, they will be able to speak with one another about all the occurrences of the day – and thereby handle or clear up arising difficulties and problems among themselves – without burdening the child or children.

So now, the father or the mother wakes the child. They not only wish their school child a good morning and a nice day, but also the teddy or the cat or doll or favorite one, which lay with the child in bed all night. A few friendly words from the mother or the father and a brief prayer of thanks for the night and for the new day, remind the small one starting school that without God the day is grey.

The child gets up, mother or father lovingly ask the following question: "Don't you have something to say to your favorite friend who slept with you?" Surely the child has something to say! It is good for the parents to remind the child of this.

Dear parents, whatever the child has to say in the early morning to its favorites, the cat, teddy or doll indicates the child's present joys of difficulties. This could perhaps shape its day and often shows the problems, but also the joys, that the day might bring. It also indicates whether the child is in harmony or disharmony.

Dear parents, it would be advisable to write down in the child's book of life the inner processes that it expresses. Among other things, these notes may give important insight already that evening or first in the following days or years, when the child reaches puberty – or, perhaps, not until it has become an adult!

After getting washed and dressed, a brief prayer should be spoken again before breakfast, if possible, with all the family members that are still at home.

It would also be good if all the family members would take a different consciousness aid or affirmation into the events of their day. At noon or in the evening they could talk about the affirmation, what effect it had and what it triggered. Affirmations are an enrichment for every family member; they can also lead to a good family conversation.

All these small and greater suggestions can, if followed, lead to a deep cohesion and unity in the family.

Some consciousness aids:

"Every person whom I meet is my neighbor."

"I find the good in my neighbor and am happy about it."

"Trees, plants and flowers radiate divine energy toward me."

"Every animal is my second neighbor. It has feelings like I do."

"The animal is life. I am life. Life feels."

The school child

School days usually run a similar course. But a school day can also bring special things if the pupil has been made aware of the positive sides of life by its parents.

If the child is not raised with didactic tones by its parents, but is guided with understanding, then the child learns to love its parents and to value its fellow people. Such children are children of the Free Spirit. They are not inhibited or tense but enjoy being active. This has a positive effect on the child's entire future life.

Therefore, the parents should remind their school child again and again that it should also understand the thinking and acting of its teachers. They often suffer under the unrestrained behavior of some school children.

Teachers also have families; a teacher is often a father or a mother. They, like the pupils, also want to take home positive impressions and memories of school.

Positive thoughts and memories trigger joy and can move the whole family to be joyful. Each and every school child can contribute to a positive and happy life by giving joy to its fellow people.

The parents of the school child should establish a good contact with the teachers and also cultivate it, so as to find out together where the light and shadowed sides of the child are, or where predispositions and characteristics for the coming choice of an occupation are recognizable.

If the child's days are largely in harmony and if no pressure or coercion is put on the child, then the child will talk a lot about itself and, without reserve or fear, talk about what pleases or displeases it and also about its difficulties. If the adults are free, open and approachable, then the child doesn't close up. The child feels understood and expresses what bothers it at any particular moment. The child feels loved, accepted and received.

Dear parents and teachers, recognize in my words your responsibility to the children who were entrusted to you. May the following also be said to the parents and teachers:

The child expresses its inner joy and current difficulties in what it draws and paints.

For this reason, I encourage parents and teachers to let the children draw or paint a lot. In school, it should be as it was in nursery school and kindergarten. The children paint and put on paper what presently preoccupies them. A child's picture often tells more than many words or an aggressive outburst.

Dear parents, keep your child's pictures! If necessary, talk about them with a good councilor.

As mentioned, whatever the child says to the teddy or doll should also be recorded in the child's book of life. It gives deep insight into the child's life.

Good parents are the best companions for their child on the way to adulthood. They will also be among the child's best friends later on when their child has grown up. So it is the parents themselves who create in their child the prerequisites, as to whether they are lonely and alone in old age – or good friends of their adult daughters and sons.

If the parents live in harmony with one another, then the child's days will also be filled with harmony.

There should be peace and security in the family, for the family is the foundation for the child's later life. In many cases, the way adults lead their life depends on the family life in which they grew up – toward becoming an independent person.

The child's world changes from day to day, from week to week, from month to month and from year to year.

The more a growing child comes into contact with its fellow people, the more clearly it senses how basically different people are. The child has become used to the world of feelings of its parents, but now in school, a completely new world opens up for the child. It now registers its schoolmates' behavior and, for the first time, experiences its sensitivity, because it senses that people often speak differently than they think. The child has to experience this itself and gradually recognize that some love it and others reject it; and the child gradually learns to endure this rejection.

So that the child doesn't become stubborn and rejecting, but remains resilient and in harmony with the inner forces, this small, still weak tree, the child, must be able to lean against the trunk of a strong tree, whose roots are firmly anchored in the inner being where the life forces are flowing. This strong tree on which the child finds support should be the family.

An intact, that is, a good, family, in which the consonance of forces and harmony determine the life of the family members, is the best foundation for the growing child.

The more the child becomes used to school, the more often it has to experience that every person thinks and feels differently, that the teachers, as well, are subject to daily fluctuations and are in different frames of mind every day or even every hour. The child will experience and also recognize the moodiness of its fellow people – and just as often have to learn and experience this on its own person. It will also experience that people who were well-disposed toward the child until now, suddenly reject it. The child will have to learn to endure oblique glances and disparaging comments from its fellow people or even from its teachers. Thereby, young people will be faced with their own stirrings and inclinations that were unknown to them until then.

Through closer encounters, whether with the teachers, or fellow pupils, or passers-by in the street, people on the bus, in the streetcar, or on the train, the growing young

person learns that everyone has different ideas and opinions. Wherever the growing young person might be, more or fewer points of reference and conversations will develop. Its own opinion, which a growing school child already has, is not always accepted by its fellow people. Differences of opinion can cause points of friction, and the pupil also has to learn that dispute and quarreling do not bring peace, but aggression, disagreements and disharmony.

The incarnated soul, the young person, will be led more and more to without, into the world, and thus, the senses of the developing youth, into the world of sensory inputs. They will slowly learn that their eyes, depending on where they roam, awaken and trigger positive or negative thoughts, desires and reactions of various kinds. Young people learn and experience on themselves that what they see can trigger disharmonies or even aggressions in them.

Ugly conversations and negative turns of speech have an effect on people's nervous system, causing them to become tense and thus contributing to further negativities.

On the other hand, positive, uplifting conversations trigger positive powers and have a harmonizing effect on the souls of both conversation partners and stimulate soul and person. Harmonious powers bring peace and balance into the inner being of a person. The inner consonance of forces in a person creates a positive interaction in the relationship between people. The harmony that emerges in a positive conversation influences the whole day. The same thing applies to eye contact. If someone likes another person, then a joyful feeling awakens in the heart, for the positive sides of the person begin to vibrate.

However, if people are not concentrated and go through the day without making efforts to discover something new each day, in order to work on themselves, then they will also see and sow much negativity – and will harvest accordingly. The nervous system will become more and more tense, and their thoughts will not contribute to the harmony and consonance of forces; neither in the family nor in the surroundings.

People who are mostly negative, that is, who feel, think, speak and act negatively, become less and less able to think and live correctly. They are pessimistic, whining and bad-tempered people who are not able to live in harmony with anything or anyone.

All these and further impressions and experiences await the school child, which grows more and more into the life on Earth, and should learn to become independent and to make its own decisions.

The law of sowing and reaping

In many cases, young people's behavior goes back to the upbringing and to the role model the parents were and are for them.

What a negative role model can cause, we can recognize by the following examples, in which schoolmates get into an argument with passers-by or streetcar passengers. If one finds fault with the other, then a fierce quarrel may start that can possibly lead to animosity, if both don't restrain themselves and don't want to see the positive in everything.

An example in a streetcar: Two passengers start an argument. Both feel attacked and quarrel with one another. While doing this, one of them stumbles into other passengers. He catches himself and holds on to a handgrip, but another passenger falls to the floor. It was only a bump, but still causes various reactions with the individual passengers. One of them holds on tightly and doesn't think about it anymore. Another is able to catch himself. A third one falls to the floor. This person now starts a fierce battle of words. He yells at the supposed culprit even though this person already apologized. He even apologizes again: "I myself was pushed and fell against you. I couldn't catch myself in time." But the upset one continues to yell – and the one who apologized, now lets himself be drawn into a vehement argument. Both parties are now in an inner turmoil: Very human, negative thoughts of anger and excitement shoot through their heads. Both send out negative "thought-seeds"; these are vibrations, and call up the same or similar vibrations in the sphere of thoughts.

The sphere of thoughts is everywhere, in the atmosphere, on the Earth – and around people who think many trivial thoughts. Everywhere, there are clusters of thoughts that people have sent and continue to send out daily, indeed, by the hour and even every minute.

The thoughts vibrate into the sphere of thoughts and trigger the same or similar thoughts.

In this way, downright concentrations of thought energies often arise that are attracted and called up. They are thus reinforced, and then come back to the senders and influence them.

It is the same way with both people arguing. The thought waves they sent out come back, now reinforced, and influence, in turn, their agitation and their words.

This means: If people are upset and not alert, and do not put their thoughts in order in good time, then their angry outburst intensifies. Then, influenced by the thought waves that come back from the sphere of thoughts, they get caught up in the situation ever more.

Through this process, both infuriated participants are shown what human aspects still lie in each of them and what they now, triggered by this situation, should recognize: what each of them ultimately still is.

Happy the people who know about the law of sowing and reaping and can hold themselves back in time from such outbursts and recognize what they have to work on themselves.

At every moment, God, the eternal power of our heavenly Father, gives soul and person the opportunity to recognize themselves in their positive or negative thoughts, whether they merely think them or speak them out, or even act upon them.

The grace of the Father flows to humankind unceasingly. At every moment, God's grace gives every single person the strength to recognize and check themselves in time – before getting upset or before some misfortune looms and breaks in over them.

For this reason, dear child, watch your thoughts!

Do not be sad when you face something that is the same or similar to what I have just described, and, you are possibly not even to blame for such an incident.

Remember: For this incident itself you may be innocent. But not for what and how you think, say or now begin to do about it!

An encounter that already happened once in a former life may have brought about this incident and now it came again on this day to the parties concerned.

Thus, an unlawful seed began to sprout that was sown into the soul in a previous life or in this life. And now it breaks open and may even bear its fruits – depending on the reaction of the ones concerned.

This incident also caused a burden to vibrate in the innocent person who got upset, also became angry, and began to fight and to express anger accordingly.

You heard correctly: According to the outburst of anger, to what broke open, the person expressed their self.

Here, I would like to put emphasis on the word "according," for human beings react according to their soul's burden. This is why I call a soul burden a correspondence.

Examine yourself, dear brother, dear sister. How would you react to such a situation?

Would you react positively, perhaps with the words: "That can happen; it's not so bad."? And do you nevertheless remain friendly and tolerant? Do your words express understanding and good will? For example: "That's alright. They didn't do it on purpose."

If you think this way, then joy and peace awaken in you. Thus, if you react in a positive way, then this incident did not meet with a correspondence in you!

Perhaps this incident stirred a memory in you. You remember a similar situation. At that time, you were very upset. Now, what happened back then no longer upsets you. This tells you that you have overcome it. Whatever a person has overcome remains merely as a memory.

From their own experiences, from the memory of what they have overcome, people gain understanding for the situation of their fellow people.

Understanding and good will bring about inner freedom and composure in a person. Composure means that they are above a situation because the same or something similar has already been overcome.

Every situation wants to tell you something!

For this reason, strive to think, speak and act prudently in every situation and in every matter. Stay calm. Be kind and understanding, even when the various incidents the day brings touch you personally. In everything that happens is also the positive! If it is possible for you to find and express the positive in everything negative, then always oppose negative thought powers with positive ones immediately. You could think and speak in the following way:

"No person is without fault.

Everyone makes mistakes and has ugly thoughts and sensations every now and then.

Therefore, I want to send good thoughts to my neighbor who wanted to hurt me and ridicule me."

If you can immediately counter hateful and envious thoughts and words with unifying thoughts of love and understanding, then it is not necessary for you to ask for forgiveness or to forgive because you – from the very first thought – thought positively!

Remember well: Those who are understanding toward their neighbor are tolerant.

To be tolerant also means: When negative things happen, think positively immediately; for example: "How often have I thought, spoken or done the same or something similar! How often did I get upset and irritated, because I disliked this or that or because my schoolmate spoke or acted differently than I wanted?

If you think in such or a similar way, you have learned from the negative situation.

Now use what you have learned, and at that, always whenever incidents remind you that it was not long ago that you, too, paid someone back in the same way!

Always endeavor to see the good in your fellow people, even when, for instance, their manners and behavior, their clothes or hairstyle displease you.

Be understanding and tolerant. Everyone is on another level of consciousness and works more or less on themselves to become selfless and divine again.

You also still have many faults and weaknesses.

No person should judge another.

If you come into a similar situation as I have just described to you, then show understanding. Smile at your neighbors and say: "Everything is okay. It wasn't so bad" – even if your neighbors laugh at you or push you away. Don't give them the opportunity to continue to think negatively about you. If you remain positive, you will not burden your soul. With your behavior, you show your neighbors how they, too, could think and act.

In any case, you did not give them a chance to produce even more thoughts of anger or even hatred. And if they still do this, it is of their own accord, but not prompted by your negative thoughts.

If you act in this way, you will neither burden your soul nor give your neighbors the opportunity to burden themselves on your account, because you behaved, thought, or spoke negatively.

If despite everything, your neighbor gets upset because of your inner calm and external bearing, because of your understanding look, then that's their business, not yours. You won't have to ask for forgiveness one day, for you did not think or speak in an ugly way.

On the other hand, the unregenerate person, who continued to send out negative thoughts and words, will have to ask your forgiveness one day. When, where and how, we will leave up to the great arbiter, the law of cause and effect, of sowing and reaping.

What is the law of sowing and reaping?

Surely you ask yourself again and again: What is sowing and reaping?

You know, dear child, that if you put a sunflower seed into the soil and frequently water it, an impressive sunflower will grow out of this little seed. A blossom will grow on a strong stem, which has many, many seeds – they are all seeds for other sunflowers.

You can experience the same thing with an apple seed. The apple seed contains all the characteristics of a mighty apple tree.

When you put an apple seed into the soil and it is watered, whether by you or the rain, then at first, a small plant emerges. It is then transplanted and the small tree that developed from it will perhaps be grafted. Over the years, this tree grows into a magnificent tree that bears many and big fruits.

These examples of the sunflower seed and the apple seed show you what sowing and reaping is. They show the positive, the good, sides of life, which a person also bears within. Just as the seeds bear within themselves the flowers, the trees and the fruits, in the same way a person bears within the predispositions for joy, peace, love and health.

However, people also have negative predispositions in themselves, such as the ugly thoughts of envy, hatred and animosity. These ugly thoughts have a destructive and poisoning effect on a person's body and lead to worry, hardship, blows of fate, illness and loneliness.

Thus, it is up to the person which thoughts are sown in the field of life, in their soul.

All a person's feelings, thoughts, words and actions are seeds that gradually germinate and grow into a person, so to speak, that is, they show their effect there and bear their kind of fruit, positive or negative. According to people's sowing, that is, according to their attitude toward life, they will reap.

When you think of thought-seeds, you can also think of the dandelion's tiny seeds, the "head" of the dandelion.

A person feels, thinks and speaks – and whatever people blow on, what is sent out by them, are seeds of life, that is, energies that we call seeds.

The good energies, the good seeds, are positive powers. So, the seeds are feelings, thoughts and words and they go to where a person sends them.

Human beings are senders of seeds. They blow them out into the environment.

Other people are the receivers of these seeds. When they feel, think, speak and act as the sender, then they absorb these energies, these seeds, that have been sent out, if the same or similar thing is present in them.

I call this the correspondences: What the sender sent out corresponds to the way the person who catches these seeds feels, thinks, speaks and acts.

Therefore, if these seeds or sprouts find a corresponding fertile soil, that is, correspondences in another person, then they settle down in that person like seeds in the soil. The fertile soil is the person and the person's soul, which are receptive to such seeds.

You already know: If something corresponding, that is, a corresponding burden, is present in the soul, then the same forces, the same seeds, will be received, because like attracts like.

It is always one's own correspondence, the soul's burden, which is the fertile soil for the negative seeds. If these seeds, these base energies, settle down in the soul of a person who absorbed them – and if they are thought by the person again and again – then with this, the person waters these seeds. These germinate and grow and bear their fruits in the person. That is, then, the harvest. It corresponds to their feelings, thoughts, words and actions.

Whatever people sow, they will reap. And whatever people sow into their neighbor's soil, they will also reap. The seed that I spread in my neighbor's field, through my positive or negative behavior, always has an effect in me, as well.

If I send out positive, selfless seeds, then I will harvest selfless energies; they are good and beautiful fruits. I will become and remain healthy, and joy and peace will be with me during my life.

On the other hand, if I send out ugly thoughts, thoughts of envy, of hatred, of animosity, then I will also harvest the same. And sooner or later, I will have to ask forgiveness of the one who took in my negative thoughts, or I will have to bear with them what I "nourished" in them.

Inculcate in yourself the path of positive and negative seeds: The positive, that is, the good, seeds, like understanding, love and tolerance fall into your field, into your soul, right away. They nourish and strengthen the soul.

The negative seeds need a longer time, because on their way to the soul the divine grace is at work, which admonishes you to change your thinking in time, to repent of what was sent out.

If you repent, then the divine grace transforms the negative forces into positive energies. However, if you remain stubborn and continue to scatter negative seeds, then the negative will continue on its way to the soul.

At first, it remains in your aura and in your conscious mind. Then it goes into the subconscious and from there, into your soul.

The negative then begins to germinate and grow in your soul, for with the same or similar thoughts, you feed everything that is in you.

The sprout then grows more and more into your world of thoughts. The thoughts of envy, of hatred, of jealousy and animosity become ever stronger. You get so angry that you can no longer hold back your words; you speak them out, and in this way, you sow discord. This leads to quarrel, strife and animosity.

Those who live in animosity with their neighbor will send them ugly thoughts again and again. They are often thoughts of revenge, for they do not want to be reconciled – because they are of the opinion that their neighbor is guilty and not them.

You know that everyone who speaks and thinks negatively is guilty and shares in the guilt. If innocent people have to suffer injustice from another and consequently harbor thoughts of revenge and retaliation, then they become guilty via these negative thoughts. Those who have experienced injustice do not want to accept this and brood on revenge, because the hateful thoughts that continue to smolder impel them to act. They stoke the fire of envy, hatred and passion to take revenge on the one who, as they assume, is solely guilty. Those who brood about revenge ultimately get the chance to strike out at their neighbor with whom they are living in animosity. They injure the others so badly that they have to go to the doctor.

You can recognize from this that both have sown a bad seed: the one who sent out the thoughts in the first place and the one who received the thoughts and continued to move them. The effect, the harvest, could be the following in this case:

Those who struck out so wildly will possibly be punished by the worldly law. The bad seed, however, which they sowed in the field of their life, in their soul – for the human being should think positively and forgive – will not be expiated with the worldly punishment.

You see: The sender of negative thoughts caused the receiver to become violent. The negative thoughts that were sent out and that fell into the soul of the other person, who then had outbursts of hatred and anger, radiate out again and into the person who sent them out in the first place.

Thus, both are bound to one another through the law of sowing and reaping as if with a cord. A so-called radiation cord is the result.

The seed that the sender sowed into the field of the receiver's soul returned manifold, because the receiver reinforced the sender's thoughts, since similar thoughts were in them, as well.

That is why it is said: Whatever you sow in thoughts, words and deeds returns to you manifold. The positive as well as the negative forces are constantly at work in the sender and the receiver.

With this radiation cord, which we could also call a thought-cord, the two in conflict are connected. Both hostile parties, the sender and the receiver, will be led together again through the law of sowing and reaping, at that time when the seed is ripe for this.

It is an act of the grace of God that allows both to meet again. Both, the sender of the negative thought energies as well as the receiver of these thoughts, are given the chance to recognize everything, to repent and to make amends for what they caused.

See, dear brothers and sisters, this is another way in which God is active, so that human beings recognize themselves, and become free of all ugly and impure thoughts, words and actions.

Free people, who are connected with God and harbor few negative thoughts, always have many good and loving friends around them.

Therefore, endeavor to be loving, in order to have good and loving friends around you. They are a great treasure for your further life. This strengthens you and gives you courage for further positive steps.

Recognize God's love and justice in these explanations. God helps us out of every situation.

However, it is better to be alert and avert the developing situation in time!

Thus, you have understood that people burden themselves ever more when they do not pay attention to their thoughts, for again and again they sow the same seed in the field of the soul and water it again and again with the same thought energies – if they are not alert.

If the seed then germinates, it then bears again the same kind of thought-seeds, like the sunflower that always has the same kind of seeds or the dandelion head that spreads only its type of seed. If thoughts are activated again and again by similar thoughts, if the same thing is thought again and again, then they fall into a person's soul in greater numbers and grow there to become the next fruit, perhaps an even bigger ugly fruit.

The sunflower and the dandelion head are the best example in the positive sense. In autumn, the sunflower seeds fall into the soil and in spring more sunflowers grow. It is similar with the dandelion head; when you blow very hard, or when the air spirits blow, then the seeds fly away and fall on the ground. In springtime, more dandelions will grow. Nature has many fitting comparisons.

Sickness, hardship and poverty in the life of a person can be the harvest of such unlawful, ugly thoughts.

Therefore, dear child, be careful to sow good thought-seeds. They go to people who are also good and continue to grow in these people. They also radiate back to you, who emits positive thoughts and words, and give you much, much energy and joy. Out of this grows the love for your fellow people. This love has understanding, good will and kindness.

You can see what good seeds do, seeds that you think and speak into the field of your neighbors' soul and thus, into your own soul. If they accept these good powers thankfully, then they effect health and peace in your neighbor – and also in you. And you will not suffer hardship, because seeds of love are positive thought energies. They help and heal and guide and connect you with others of like mind, that is, with good people.

Someone who sows seeds of good will, of peace and love will never be lonely or alone, because positive, loving thoughts connect those people who think and live selflessly.

Certainly, you would also like to be a positive person. It is up to you. Come and accept it; begin and achieve!

For you now know that your thoughts are the seeds, and the harvest is what is in and on you and has an effect around you.

You have recognized that the one to blame for misfortune, suffering, sickness and need is not another, your neighbor but that you yourself are the perpetrator. You have sent out negative, that is, unloving, thought-seeds either in this life or in one of your former lives. While these negative seeds germinated, you hardly felt anything. Like the seed that lies in the soil for a longer period of time before it begins to germinate, so it is with the thought-seeds that fall into the field of the soul. It can take a long time, perhaps even one or two lives on Earth, until the seed germinates and the person harvests its fruits. During that time, however, God's grace knocks constantly at your heart and says to you: "You don't have to bear your negative seeds as fruits on your body; you don't have to endure worries, fear, blows of fate and hardship. Come now and be good. Repent, love God and your neighbor, then I, the great Giver, God in you, will transform much, so that you do not have to bear it." That is the Father's grace.

But you, dear child, have to take the first step toward our Father and toward your Redeemer, our Father's Son. The first step is: Endeavor to live in peace, friendship and harmony with everyone and not to let your thoughts fly around uncontrolled here and there. Consider well what you think and speak – and take back the negative thoughts. Speak to your eternal Father: "Lord, You love me. I, too, want to love my fellow people, no matter what they say, what they do or what they talk about."

Those who love God can also love their parents and grandparents, their brothers and sisters and friends. Begin by taking this first step and you will feel great joy in your heart.

The effects of positive thoughts, words and also actions are manifold: You will have great joy and you will accomplish much. You will not have any great difficulties in school. You will learn more easily, because joy will invigorate your brain cells and all your body cells more strongly. That also means that you will be able to concentrate better and absorb the learning material more easily.

God helps, accept this!

On the other hand, those who are preoccupied solely with themselves can concentrate on their work with much more difficulty. They are often clouded with their own thoughts.

This can make life as an adult more difficult. Such a person can lose their employment or can be lonely and desolate and not find any friends, because they think solely of themselves.

I want to warmly recommend to you once more how you can protect yourself against negative thoughts.

Always think positively about your fellow people.

You don't want your friends to think negative, that is, ugly, thoughts about you. So don't do this either!

You also wish that your teachers like you, that they don't scold you, but praise you.

So, ask yourself: Do you like your teachers? Do you send them love energies, that is, love-seeds, which connect you with them and which bring joy?

Be the one who begins first! Bring joy!

Do not ask whether your teacher will also do this. You, send out good thoughts! And then many good thoughts – and lots of love – will come to you.

Never expect others to begin first. But trust in the law of love.

Whatever a person sows, they will reap.

When? When the time is ripe for this. Just as the sunflower and the apple seed need their time to germinate, to grow or to blossom and bear fruit, so it is, too, with thought energies, with thought-seeds.

Dear school child, the way to school today brought you new knowledge again.

You met many people again. You looked into totally different faces than you did yesterday or the day before.

You say that the people are strangers to you.

I ask you: Are they really strangers?

If you look only at the exterior of a person, then this person is a stranger to you.

You have, for example, never before seen a particular person whom you met on your way. That means that you saw the person's present earthly garment for the first time. However, you know the spirit being, the soul that lives in this strange person. It is your brother or sister and a child of the Kingdom of God as you also are.

It is not by chance that you meet different people every day or the same ones every now and then!

The law of life says: Endeavor to love all people whom you meet.

If you get upset about someone and begin to think ugly and unkind thoughts about them, then the law of life is giving you a hint via this person: Reflect about your thoughts and clear out immediately the negativity this encounter triggered in you. At the same time, through Christ, you should ask forgiveness of this person and the soul about which you had ugly and unkind thoughts.

You see, in this way, even your way to school can become a "path of recognition," if you are attentive and watch yourself again and again!

Surely you are now asking whether you can love people who don't love you, or whether you can love your schoolmates who ridicule you, or even those who have already hit you, or whether you can love your teacher who has scolded you unjustly. You can certainly do this!

Don't say that they don't like you because they have hit you or that your teacher scolded you unjustly.

The human being likes to say: The other one is guilty and I am innocent!

But you know now: It's not that simple!

Think about the seed, about the correspondences, the shadows of your soul!

The shadows, the correspondences, that is, the seeds in your soul, are a magnetic field. They attract exactly what you yourself caused in this life on Earth or in one of your former lives and that are not yet atoned for. Thus, there are still dark spots on your soul. If they were atoned for, then there would no longer be shadows in you – and you would not get upset and blame your neighbor.

If there is nothing negative left in your soul, that is, no more negative seeds, no shadows, then it is no longer at all possible that your schoolmate hits you or that your teacher wrongs you!

If it happens anyway, and you don't get upset, but remain understanding and calm and correct this misunderstanding – then this was merely a temptation for you. However, you didn't succumb to it. But if you get upset and look for the blame for this behavior in your tempter, then you have succumbed to the temptation. Your still-present shadows have reacted accordingly and you struck back angrily using the same or similar words as your tempter.

You should now ask yourself what is still in *you*!

Every agitation is based on a human aspect in yourself.

Examine yourself: Why were you angry or fearful and what ugly thoughts did you have? What nasty words did you use?

From this, you can recognize what is in you.

Perhaps you got angry because you recognized that it is exactly as your "tempter" said – or that what the other person triggered in you merely through the encounter is right, and you simply don't want to accept this.

Or you are afraid because you had nasty, that is, ugly, thoughts and the "tempter" sees you as you are, and you now assume that the tempter can even read your thoughts.

Thus, examine your thoughts and words.

And examine your senses very closely.

What did you see that made you upset?

What did you hear that made you afraid?

What did you smell that was pleasant or unpleasant – and called forth sensations of envy or stimulated you to use ugly words?

The sense of taste and touch can also cause the shadows of your soul to vibrate.

As you know, the five senses are the antennas that stimulate memories and correspondences in you.

There are many possibilities to stimulate your senses.

Perhaps your schoolmate has a good snack that you would like to have. Perhaps your school friend was praised by the teacher or was given a task that you would like to have done?

Every discontentment in a person, envy, anger, fear, or rage against others are reactions of one's own soul.

Every discontentment shows what is taking place in the person and what still lies in the soul.

All these external occasions can address the conscious mind, the subconscious and the soul's shadows. These then begin to vibrate and trigger corresponding reactions in a person.

You now know these principles of the law.

How do you now face yourself when you have recognized yourself?

To face yourself means: To see yourself as you really are.

Your feelings and thoughts show how you are. Whatever you feel and think is what you are. Examine and recognize yourself in this.

It is not only your neighbor who angers you. Anyone who triggered the anger in you was merely a helper of the cosmic law, to show you what you are still lacking. At the same time, they were given the opportunity to recognize themselves in their behavior.

If you remain calm within despite your neighbor's attacks, then you can set the incident right in all composure and calmness, and place the incident in the hands of God, our heavenly Father – no matter how your neighbor reacts.

If you show understanding and the right love, you have long since overcome what was said or done to you. There may be only a memory left in your soul – or you have never caused the same or something similar. What someone said to you or did to you was then a temptation through the tempter, the darkness in this world.

Dear child, never separate yourself from your fellow classmates. And don't be an impudent child, a so-called know-it-all, who shows off and thinks it knows everything better than others. Apply on yourself first whatever you know and have recognized. Then you will not boast about your knowledge. Knowledge should become wisdom.

Truly wise people do not boast, because they have experienced much themselves and have overcome it with the strength of the Lord. They contribute their experiences to the community or convey them to individuals, but they do not impose their experiences on anyone. At the right time and in the right moment, they give what is essential, that means, what the soul of the person concerned needs, not what the human being wants to hear or have.

The guardian angel of those who are wise, that is, who live in the law of God, is very near to them and helps and supports them in every situation. If, however, you want to boast about your knowledge, then your guardian angel withdraws more and more, because it is not asked, but rather the human being, the boaster, only wants to reveal their knowledge, so as to be praised or admired. Anyone who strives for praise and recognition will receive praise, reward and recognition from this world, and not from God, our heavenly Father.

Therefore, whoever has received reward, praise and recognition from this world has already been rewarded. The guardian angel will not help either, because the boaster already has the reward and is satisfied with it.

You now know how you can behave, so that you have a true friendship with the teachers and schoolmates. Show-offs, also called boasters, are quickly recognized by their teachers and fellow pupils and pushed aside, because no one likes know-it-alls. Since they are constantly focused on lecturing others, they can hardly develop a warm relationship with their fellow people. It is also not much fun to play with show-offs. They frequently interrupt the game and think they know everything better.

Become wise, but do not be a know-it-all.

The school lessons

Be attentive during class.

I have already explained to you how important it is to concentrate on one thing.

Many, many thoughts are constantly darting through a person's head. Human beings think unceasingly – and think all sorts of things if they have not learned to concentrate.

But someone who has practiced concentration is attentive. Learn to concentrate!

For example, while you are concentrating on a certain activity, if an important thought or a good idea occurs to you that has nothing to do with your present work, then don't move it! Do not allow yourself to be distracted from your present work!

Write down this important thought, or idea, or recognition; then continue your work. For you, this means: Follow the school lesson again.

Most of all, be free of ugly thoughts. Then you will be a good pupil.

Dear parents, how can you encourage your children's concentration?

Every child is more or less distracted by the outside world, children in the cities more so than children in towns and villages. People's senses are always ready to register everything that comes to them, and to distract the human being. This is especially true when a soul bears greater burdens.

Soul burdens developed and develop through a behavior that is against God's laws.

Feelings and thoughts develop in a person through the senses – whether the person has them under control or not. These trigger – in a kind of chain reaction – corresponding reactions in the soul as well as in the conscious mind and the subconscious of the person, and cause further thoughts and pictures and are either positive, that is, selfless, or negative, that is, egocentric.

Anyone who does not get their senses under control burdens themself again and again – and, depending on the burden, can already determine the path for their next incarnation.

The senses address the energies that vibrate in the soul and in the subconscious and the conscious mind.

However, they also attract from the sphere of thoughts nice, that is, lawful thoughts, or ugly, that is, unlawful, thoughts.

Anyone who moves unlawful thoughts within for a longer period of time can also call up burdening thoughts from the sphere of thoughts that then influence them.

Dear parents, explain these lawful correlations to your children in your own way, with your own words, that the children are used to and can understand.

No later than the first year of school, the parents and the teachers should explain to the child about vibrations and how the senses work: that everything is vibration and that the senses can call up positive as well as negative vibrations.

The magnet for the positive, for the good and selfless forces as well as for the negative, egocentric forces is in the human being. It is their burdened soul and their subconscious and conscious mind.

So that people can learn to concentrate, their senses should gradually obey them.

Dear parents, learning can be a game for children when parents and teachers are able to be responsive to the child's psyche.

I assume that parents and teachers have an understanding for this.

My revelation shows how a child can learn concentration and receptivity in a playful way. At the same time, this can be an exercise for the parents.

When your child comes home from school make sure to greet the child warmly.

The child should feel free and secure at home. It should be able to open up according to its nature and express everything that is joyful, burdening and depressing.

If the child is given the opportunity and the time for this, then the child's subconscious will not store too many negative and depressive things – and burden the child. And the conscious mind will then remember more of the positive, and store what is important.

The training of the senses can be an important factor in the lawful upbringing of positive people.

The child should be able to relax after school. It should – but it doesn't have to! The child can also find relaxation and peace at a place or in an activity to which it feels drawn.

After the period of rest, the child will do its homework.

Afterward in the evening or on a free day – when the parents have time and the child is willing – another important part of learning begins – not only for the years in school but for the entire life, for a later occupation and for everyday life. It is the training of the senses. This training can be done in a playful way. It is instructive for both parents and children.

Games for Training the Senses, Concentration and Self-recognition

A game with the senses

Dear parents, first of all, some good advice: When you begin with this "game of the senses," then begin with the sense of sight, for the eyes have the strongest effect on all the other senses.

Every participant has paper and pencil in front of them. One player asks everyone the question:

To where does our sense of sight urge us? What do we see at this moment and what are we thinking at the same time?

The looks of each player will be drawn to where they are directed by their sense of sight – or of hearing.

During this "game of the senses," every player should be relaxed.

The players shouldn't focus on any one object. They just let things happen and look to where their eyes are drawn.

Then each player writes down what they saw and simultaneously thought.

If the children still find it difficult to write, they quietly tell the result to the mother or father who then writes down the child's words. The child of the first and possibly also of the second school year may have a doll or a teddy or a cat or another favorite on its lap or sitting next to it.

Why should this favorite toy be present? If the child cannot take notes yet, and the parents do this for the child, then the child needs a point of reference. That is its favorite toy. The point of reference for the adult who writes down what they saw and thought is the piece of paper. They focus their attention there and concentrate on what they write.

For the child that just started school, the focal point is the doll, the teddy, or another favorite toy. The child that still has difficulty writing tells the parents what the child saw and thought or what the doll or the teddy has to say.

When all players are finished taking their notes, they briefly say what they saw, to where their eyes turned and which thoughts rose up.

Mother or father read what the child starting school whispered to them. What the favorite toy, teddy or cat had to report by way of the child will also be read aloud.

Now it gets interesting!

Why did the one look here and the other look there?

Who or what attracted their eyes? And why are their thoughts not always related to what they saw?

If the thoughts are not related to what was seen, then whatever attracted the sense of sight touched the powers of thought in the subconscious or in the soul garments. These pushed up into the conscious mind and became thoughts and words.

This means that the sense of sight is drawn uncontrolled here and there, and that the person is not able to register what happens at a particular moment, because there is something unresolved in their inner being.

What the sense of sight registered, thus calls up from the subconscious or the conscious mind – or from the soul garments – past incidents or thoughts that have consciously or unconsciously influenced the person. This shows that the person is not yet free and that what the eye perceived cannot totally be concentrated upon.

Such people often think and speak about something totally different than what the eye conveys to them.

Therefore, adults and children are not free as long as they cannot concentrate on what they see – but call up other things from the sphere of thoughts, from the soul garments or from the conscious mind or subconscious.

The adults can then talk about the various components of what was seen and what was thought.

Everyone can ask themselves the question: What's going on with me? What have I not overcome yet? What needs to be forgiven or where should I request forgiveness? Mother or father should help the child find out what is going on in the child.

The test with the senses has the effect that unconscious inner processes often become active and reach the conscious mind. Then, they can be cleared up before they become evident as effects in and on the body.

For the children there could be another step.

They draw what they saw with their eyes – and which thoughts they had as a result.

When both pictures are then compared, what the child saw and what the child thought, this gives a deeper insight into the inner life of the child.

A trained life councilor can conclude much from such an exercise. Abilities and talents concerning a later choice of occupation can also be recognized here.

The parents are advised to deal carefully with what was said and drawn. In later years, when the child is an adult, it can be a great help for the continuing years of life.

The game with the senses can be very joyful and instructive – for children as well as for adults.

When what was seen corresponds for the most part with the thoughts, then the child can concentrate and, at present, has no great problems; the conscious mind and the subconscious are not burdened with grave thought complexes.

With this game, all five senses can be tested.

Each time is shown to what extent the conscious mind and the subconscious, or even the soul garments of a player are burdened.

This "game of recognition" shows further components of the human ego through the senses of hearing, smell, taste and touch.

It is certainly interesting and instructive for the players to recognize which thoughts or even thought-complexes begin to vibrate that they become aware of. If, for example, they perceive the sounds of autos, listen to the singing of birds, or when they look at flowers and smell the fragrance of the blossoms.

Just as instructive is, for instance, when they smell a roast in the oven, which thoughts and ideas come up.

The same is true for the sense of touch. Which feelings and thoughts are called up when a player touches, for example, walls, furniture or fabrics.

The game of the senses should be played totally casually, without any programming. Don't expect, dear player, that when, for instance, you see a flower or smell a blossom that you absolutely have to think of the flower or its fragrance.

The "game of the senses" should show you what's going on in you, what you really still are!

For what people think is what they are.

Your senses stimulate your thoughts, which means that they set a lot of things free which, as already revealed, lie latent in your conscious mind or subconscious – or even in your soul garments.

Just as the adults, the mother, the father or the teacher help the child learn to concentrate, they can also help themselves.

The adults ask themselves why their sense of sight, or their sense of smell, touch or taste led them here or there and why the thoughts that came up digress from this.

These questions to yourself can break open the thought-complex that can tell what lies in your inner being – and which causes could be the reason for not having been able to concentrate. The questions you ask yourself automatically activate the world of feelings and thoughts. The "sensitivity level" lies under the layers of the thought level – that is, in the world of feelings. This sensitivity level is also touched by the guardian spirit. It is our conscience. The divine lies under the layers of the soul burdens. It can penetrate into the conscious mind and communicate itself only once we are spiritually developed and attentive, that is, when our senses are refined and obey us.

In this "game of the senses," the parents can learn what lies in the child's world of feelings when they ask the child, but also the doll, teddy or cat that are also present at the game and can also report many things. For the child not only communicates its thoughts to its parents but also to a favorite toy.

Every thought and every word is energy.

Energy adheres to where it is thought or spoken. Therefore, with the child, it adheres to the teddy, the doll, the cat or some other favorite toy.

Encouraged by the parents, the child now questions its favorite toy: What does teddy think about why the child thought about other things instead of what the eyes or ears conveyed to the child?

This question from the child – directed to the favorite toy – triggers a thought-complex there that may consist of joy or sorrow, which – in a joyful or sad situation, in sorrow or pain – the child has built up around its teddy, because the child let its feelings, thoughts or words, that is, energies, flow to the teddy. These feelings, thoughts and words are energies. They adhere to the teddy and become an energy-complex there.

If this energy – or thought-complex is addressed, it begins to vibrate and communicates itself via the child's feelings and thoughts. This takes place as follows:

Every joyful or painful feeling emitted by a person creates a magnetic field in the person which, in turn, attracts the same vibration.

The energy field, the energy-complex around the teddy, connects itself with the energy-complex in the child and communicates itself in this way via the conscious mind. It is the well-known "Ah, now I remember" or: "My eyes were opened."

The favorite toys, the doll, teddy or the cat, are alive for the child, not stiff, lifeless figures. The child feels that the doll, cat or teddy move, that they speak, that they do this or that. They live and send back what the child felt, thought and spoke to them before.

I repeat:

The "movements and expressions" of the favorite toys are the joys, difficulties, problems, sorrows, pain, fear and worries that have been felt, thought and spoken into them by the child.

The question regarding what the favorite toy may have to say about this or that incident sets into motion vibrations in the favorite toy as well as in the child, and the favorite toy begins to speak through the child. The child says, for example: The teddy or the doll said this or that. That is what is in the child and what the child has spoken or thought into the teddy or the doll. In this way, the child expresses what is present in its inner being, what has not been overcome and what contributed, or still contributes, to the lack of concentration: The child expresses it own joys and sorrows.

Good parents recognize this well. With the child, they strive to playfully clear up what burdens the child and in later years could cause more far-reaching consequences or even physical harm.

A game for training the concentration

 give more games to train the self-recognition and also to learn concentration.

These games conveyed by me, Liobani, for concentration, lawful thinking and, at the same time, self-recognition are instructive for all who are open and without expectations of themselves, who want to work on themselves and be selfless players. Each player writes down one or more sentences, whatever comes to mind. Then each one reads what they wrote and at the same time, asks themself and their world of feelings whether what they wrote down is in accord with their world of feelings.

The world of feelings transmits to the questioner either a good, a positive or less-good, negative feelings.

Thus, whatever the players thereupon feel, they let come into their world of thoughts and write it down.

If bland feelings rise out of the world of sensations or if the player becomes restless, sad or even bad tempered, then they can be sure that something unconscious lies behind this.

What can it be?

To explore the deeper reasons, the player endeavors to question the world of their own senses and feelings. If they direct this question to their world of the senses and feelings without reservations or an exaggerated opinion of themself, it is possible that all of a sudden, a light goes on: "Now I have it; it can be only this or that."

The scales fell from their eyes, as it were.

What happened?

Via the world of feelings, impulses rose out of the realm of the unconscious, triggered by the question to the world of the senses and feelings regarding what was going on inside them, the person.

Everyone can recognize themselves through such or similar games of the senses and thoughts.

While the adult takes notes, the child can draw if it still has difficulty writing. The child's drawings have the same informative value as the adult's notes. If a great gap exists between what a player thinks and what they feel, if their world of thoughts differs a great deal from their world of feelings, then this person has a split personality that is not quite able to think, speak and feel. These dissonances and discrepancies lead to difficulties in school as well as in their occupation and in the family.

The soul of a human being is not of this world. It is constantly striving to communicate with the person, with the "vehicle" of the soul. And this is why a person can have an intuition at any moment, if the senses are trained and if the person is practiced in concentration. True intuition, the feeling and the true inspiration, the revelation, comes from God. If a person does not want anything of their own accord, nor has any expectations of their neighbor, rather allowing the unending, eternal, free powers to work in themselves, then guidance begins from within.

Important steps on the path within to selfless, radiating love are the prerequisite for true intuition and revelation.

The guide on this path to the true self are:

Put *Order* in your thoughts; cleanse and spiritualize your senses and clear up your past.

Whatever you expect of your neighbor do it yourself first.

Not your will should take place, but God's *Will*.

Not your knowledge should be actualized, but the *Wisdom* of the eternal Father.

Your life should not be easy-going but *Earnest*, which means conscious, goal-oriented and selfless.

In the same way that people expect *Patience* from their neighbor, they should also have patience with their neighbor!

Out of this grow selfless *Love* and *Mercy*.

In a few short words, that is the Inner Path to true intuition and revelation.

It is important and essential for a person's later life to attain divine input, divine intuition.

This is, however, possible only if a person no longer condemns or judges, if they do not expect recognition, but live selflessly. Only then, will they gain intuition from high, pure planes.

Everything else, every seeming input, can either come from the person, themselves, or be called up from the atmospheric chronicle or be given by souls out of the astral planes.

Therefore, may everyone examine their basic attitude, their thinking and wanting, before letting their intuition lead them.

This game that I have revealed brings about self-recognition and inner freedom in a person – insofar as they learn to overcome everything that they have recognized in the right way, that is, step by step.

A child learns concentration through this. This means that it practices concentrating on one thing.

It is a great help for the child in school as well as in its further life on Earth, for a choice of occupation and in the occupation.

If a young person is trained in this way, then, as an adult, they can think correctly, speak concentratedly and act consciously. This leads to a positive, happy and fulfilled life.

Such a person faces life in an affirmative manner. They think positively and also work with the positive powers. They are balanced and concentrated, filled by the consciousness: What I do, I do totally.

Because they already began as children to master their lives, such people are happy and content and fulfilled by their activity, which corresponds to their nature and mentality. This means that they are alert people who immediately survey each situation, grasp it correctly and are also able to deal with it. They are not loners. They do not isolate themselves. Nor will they be loners, hermits or fanatics. Their subconscious and their soul are not burdened with unimportant and self-centered things; they are undemanding. They have learned to think and act correctly, that is, to live correctly; this shapes them their whole life long. Such people are people of action. Their past does not burden them, since day by day they correctly grasp their life, that is, their thoughts and feelings, and direct these into lawful channels.

They have already learned and practiced this during their childhood. They are free, happy and healthy people – people of the New Era.

Not every person can affirm these teachings and playful exercises; for many, what is written here is still foreign to them, or, from the outset, they view what is given in revelation very skeptically.

Dear friends, before you put this book aside, however, with such or similar human reactions, it should be worthwhile to at least try to read it.

Without reservation, try out the teachings, the lessons and the games with the senses. Only then, will it be possible for you to make a judgment about it!

Keep in mind, however, that people are on different consciousness levels and that everyone classifies and understands spiritual knowledge according to their own spiritual development.

Dear brother, dear sister, are you always ready to help your neighbor, your fellow people, when they need your help and when they ask for it? Are you always good to all animals and do you also respect the life of plants, of herbs, flowers, bushes and trees, as well as that of stones?

Think about this and talk it over with your parents and brothers and sisters.

If you are not always ready to help your neighbor, your fellow people, and also to meet your second neighbors, the animals, plants and stones, in love, then you should ask yourself why not, and what prevents you from helping and serving selflessly – like the spirit beings and the elemental beings.

Surely you can talk with your father or mother or with one of your brothers and sisters about what prevents you from doing this. Much can be recognized and much can also be rectified in conversation.

With this, I, Liobani, encourage a family conversation that can become very interesting when all family members take part. The conversation can include the following topics:

What is in me that prevents me from helping selflessly?

What is in you that prevents you from serving selflessly?

How can we family members change this and in what way can we help each other?

Someone who gives selflessly receives much strength from our heavenly Father, so as to help and serve people who need help and also want help.

Selfless people look at all other people in the light of truth, because they know that all people are children of God.

People with a great selfless love in their hearts also sense how they can help God's creatures, the animals and plants.

Dear brother, dear sister, how do you attain selflessness?

Always remember that in all people, no matter how they think, speak and act, there is also a good and beautiful core. Look for this and find it!

In this way, your life will become or remain positive, friendly and happy.

The animals, plants and stones also have good qualities. Search and find these and be happy about them. Then it will become bright in you. You can meet all people in a friendly way and you will also radiate toward the animals, plants and stones.

A game of insight

Now I give you another game for the family. It helps to recognize yourself and to gain unity in the family, with all people and life forms. The game goes like the following:

Each family member, one after the other, looks for the good and endearing core in another family member. Then they all talk about it. Whatever they felt in their hearts, they write down.

Once the players have noted down their feelings, then they talk about them, how these feelings are expressed in their inner being and in their body; for instance, as joy, thankfulness or peace, and how they now perceive their neighbor, in whom they found the good core.

After this collective recognition within the family, the game of insight continues.

The family members look and find the good core in a neighbor, in their school friends, the teachers and colleagues at work.

If this game of insight is played honestly, then each will realize that among the people there is so much that is good and endearing, which is sometimes still hidden under the hard shell of the human ego.

Whoever learns to frequently address what is good breaks open the hard shell of the human ego, so that the good core becomes visible – in themselves and in their neighbor.

Dear players of the "game of insight," you should address the good that was recognized in you and in your neighbor, again and again. This causes a warm and friendly contact and creates a reciprocal trust.

The game of finding good and useful things can also be continued with animals and plants. It is also possible with minerals and stones, for everything that lives bears in itself the divine, the good.

This game links the family members with each other, and in addition, produces a connection with other people. In the same way, people also regain access and a connection to animals, plants and stones.

The players will learn that everything lives and radiates, and that life feels, no matter through which form it shows itself. All people who are willing to discover and overcome their own mistakes, thus draw closer to God, our heavenly Father, who is the Creator of all life forms and the All-Spirit of infinity.

To deepen your spiritual knowledge, I repeat: The heavenly Father is the manifestation out of the flowing life energy, the primordial energy, the Spirit.

This therefore means that our heavenly Father has the form of a pure spirit being. His radiation, however, exceeds that of all spirit bodies, because He is the highest form of light in the universe.

The Creator-God is the Spirit, also called the All-Spirit. It is the breath of life of the heavenly Father. Out of this breath, out of the Spirit, all spiritual forms emerged and emerge.

Only once a matured nature being has developed all the four elemental spheres and has grasped these in their consciousness – that is, has lived through them – do they become a spirit child. They become a spirit being, the image of our heavenly Father.

A spirit being that has accepted and received the attributes of our heavenly Father, who is Mother at the same time – Patience, Love and Mercy – is then fully matured and has absolute free will.

Only once the three attributes, Patience, Love and Mercy are fully active in the spirit child, is it then the image of the eternal Father and a matured child of God.

All other life forms that are not yet images of the Father feel the All-Power as their life's spirit and serve the All-Spirit, the Spirit of life, which is in them as the evolutionary power, as it were, on the way to the Father-filiation relationship.

Once you have heard and read all of this, you have much knowledge from the divine Wisdom.

However, knowledge alone does not make people wise and kind.

Only the actualization of all that you know, that is, the right application in your life, makes a wise and kind person out of someone who knows.

The foundation is knowledge. However, don't let the foundation of knowledge become too great, by merely accumulating knowledge. Instead, transform this knowledge and what you have recognized into Wisdom: Apply what you have recognized to yourself. Then you can build on the foundation of knowledge and thus become ever richer in knowledge – and increase in wisdom.

You have already heard of boasters. The following should be said about this:

Truly wise people do not boast. They are always ready to help their neighbor as much as possible according to their possibilities and capabilities. They will neither ask for wages nor expect recognition, but will do what is good and helpful according to the law of selfless love.

Only those people boast about their knowledge who do not put this knowledge into practice. Such people are not readily accepted and received. They are the so-called know-it-alls, who grate on the nerves of those who are forbearing and tolerant. Therefore, do not be a know-it-all or a showoff, that is, a boaster. Instead, strive to apply the knowledge on yourself, to try it out and experience it. Then you will become understanding, tolerant and kind to all people. In school, it will then be much easier for you to accept and understand the teacher's lessons and homework assignments.

The wise person is also a spiritually prudent person who is capable of thinking clearly and also acting conscientiously.

Thus, wise people are spiritually prudent people with a clear mind. They can concentrate and quickly grasp much of what is said to them. At the same time, they also have a solution that corresponds to the divine laws. Such prudent people exist!

Dear child, do you also want to become such a spiritually prudent person?

If yes, then strive to be honest and friendly to all people. It will be possible for you, if you have found the good core of your neighbor and also speak about it.

A feigned friendliness is falsity. As time passes, it brings you only vexation.

Truly wise people find the good in every person.

In this way, they find their way to divine wisdom and spiritual prudence more and more. From this, results true friendliness and spiritual greatness. Truly wise people, spiritually prudent ones, are above human shortcomings. They have learned to correctly feel, to think, to speak and to act. Therefore, become wise and prudent!

When you are in school, be attentive.

Strive to participate in the lesson. Recognize, too, that your teacher honestly strives to make the lesson understandable for you.

Speak only when you know what to say. Speak clearly without wanting to show off. This also leads to understanding, tolerance and kindness.

If something bothers you, do not just brood about it, but talk about it with your parents or also with your doll or teddy or the cat. In that way, you stay free from brooding, aimless and unimportant thoughts, and your brain and subconscious remain clear for important things, like lessons, homework or other tasks and obligations that the day brings.

If you frequently do the concentration exercises as a game with your parents and brothers and sisters, then you will reach and retain clarity in your thoughts and actions.

Now, dear brother, dear sister, you are getting older! You have heard from me the word duty. You have already heard a lot in school and also from me, your spiritual sister, Liobani. And now you can already take on small duties!

What could these duties be like?

You can start by washing and dressing yourself alone. If until now you haven't already done this, then practice this! Your mother will be very happy! Exercises for developing a sense of duty also stimulate selflessness, and that, when you take on smaller and greater duties joyfully.

At the breakfast table, you can, for example, pass the marmalade or the butter to your brothers and sisters.

Or, during the course of the day, after school, for instance, you can run small errands or help in the garden. There are so many small things that have to be done and surely you are already capable of doing some of them. In this way, you gradually get used to becoming an independent person, who is able to organize their life more and more on their own. You can also make your parents happy with this, relieving them of many daily tasks and helping them to the extent possible according to your age and understanding – that is, according to your spiritual prudence. Note well: according to your spiritual prudence, that is, your wisdom, not just based on your knowledge.

Wise and prudent people are pleasant people. They are attentive, alert and quiet. They help when they are needed. They don't urge their help on others. But they are there, ready to selflessly help and to serve according to their possibilities. Therefore, become spiritually prudent and with a sense of duty. Then you will become a citizen of the new, light-filled age.

Dear brothers and sisters, you are becoming older and more mature.

You have already walked the way to school many times. Each time, you meet other people. You have also taken in different impressions each time.

The lesson hours have become more varied. In the meantime, you have learned to write, to read and to calculate.

Surely you have already had lessons in history and have heard many things about the life and thinking of people who lived on Earth before you.

You also now know, dear brother, dear sister, that every person has an indwelling soul, a spirit body, living within them.

The soul, the indwelling spirit body, is in the physical body in order to atone, in the shortest time possible, for the soul-debt that a person inflicted on themselves in earlier lives or in this life. It is, however, also possible that a soul has come into an earthly body to fulfill a divine task.

Both the burdened soul and the soul, which is in a human body to fulfill a divine task, are commanded to *love God above all else and their neighbor as themselves.*

Thus, you are here on Earth to become as selfless and loving as you were in heaven and as all the angels are, the divine beings. Therefore, this is your task in your earthly garment.

So that you can fulfill this task, new tasks are given to you each day.

The day's light irradiates the human being and the soul and in this way, has the effect that on each day, each person receives what should be overcome, what should be cleared up on that day.

The tasks are different for every person. They receive them from the daily occurrences all according to their soul's burden. Pay attention to which tasks the energy of the day addresses in you.

God is the light of the day. He is also active in the daily occurrences.

He gives you your tasks by way of the law of sowing and reaping. What you once sowed, the good, the less good and the bad seed, all sprouts in the field of life, in your soul. What you do not repent of in time then has an effect in and on your body. In every seed, in the good as well as in the less good or in the bad seed, is the Spirit, the life, which brings to light what is good, less good and bad.

Therefore, on each day, in every hour and minute, every person is given the possibility to recognize themselves and to make amends in good time for what they caused, that is, sowed. In each of your sensations, in each thought, in each word and in each action, God shows you who you are. Whatever you feel, think, speak and do, that is what you are.

At the same time, the Spirit of our heavenly Father and your guardian angel stimulate your conscience, so that on each day you can recognize what you should clear up now and today.

God, our heavenly Father, and your guardian angel stimulate you to positive thinking, speaking and acting. Through your teachers, through your school friends, they show you what is active in you and in your soul as light and shadow.

Through your parents, grandparents and relatives, God also shows you your good, less good and bad sides.

In like manner, God shows you through fellow people in traffic, on the street or in stores what is still lacking in you – or what you have already overcome, that is, made amends for.

If, for example, your teacher reprimands you or your schoolmates blame you for something and you think this is not right, then check your reaction.

As soon as you get upset, react strongly and angrily justify yourself, you can be sure that there is something in you that is not in order. You are stung by the teacher's reprimand or your schoolmates' accusation. Whoever has been stung cries out.

God can also address you in this way through your teacher or schoolmates, and show you with this that there is still something in you which you should think about, in order to clear it up immediately.

Every strong agitation gives information and hints about what is going on in a person who gets upset, about their faults and weaknesses.

If you do not get upset, then you can be sure that there is nothing in you or merely still traces of what was addressed by others.

If you remain calm within, despite your teacher's reprimands or your schoolmates' accusations, then you can be sure that there is nothing in this regard or merely very little that is still in you.

Someone who is not stung will set the reprimand and accusations straight and then let the matter rest.

If you are above the reprimands or accusations, that is, if you don't get upset, then it won't make much difference to you when the teachers or the schoolmates persist with their opinions. You know that it is not as it was presented. You have set it straight and then left it as it is, even if, for the moment, it seems as if the teacher or the schoolmates were right. Know that everything that is untrue comes to light. It will be clarified through the power of God. If you know this, then you attain firmness of thought, word and deed.

Therefore, dear brother, dear sister, you can recognize yourself each day, each hour, each minute and each second, in order to then master the day correctly.

I now give you another game of insight.

Ask your parents, brothers and sisters or schoolmates whether they want to play with you.

Every player puts a small notebook and a pencil or pen either in their schoolbag or in their pocket.

Each player watches the day via their thoughts and words to determine whether what they think are also their sensations and whether their words also correspond to their thoughts.

If they are addressed, then they should watch and check whether their words or thoughts correspond to their sensations.

After having given an answer or after a conversation, they immediately take their notebook and pencil or pen and note down:

What did I think while I was speaking?

What did I feel regarding the questioner or the conversation partner?

You will recognize very quickly that your feelings and thoughts are not always in accord with what you say.

Why is this so?

This can have various causes:

Perhaps you want to make a good impression on your conversation partner, because you expect them to do something for you.

Or you want praise and recognition from them.

Or you are afraid of them.

Or you have an inferiority complex.

All these are causes that make you speak other than what you feel and think.

Realize that to think other than you feel and to speak other than you think causes uneasiness and inner conflict in your life.

It is then no longer possible for you to think clearly and to correctly concentrate on the conversation or on other things, because your conscious mind and subconscious are gradually crammed with fearful, pessimistic, doubting and brooding thought complexes.

With every impulse that has the same vibration as this complex, your conscious mind and subconscious become more active and affect your feeling, thinking and speaking. It doesn't allow you to speak as you feel and think anymore. This discrepancy also has an effect in school and later in your occupational life. These negative complexes in your conscious mind and subconscious also have an effect on your nervous system and on your organs. You can become nervous and possibly sick.

Therefore, if through this game you recognize that you feel differently than you think, and speak differently than you feel and think, then ask yourself why this is so and what you should clear up, so that you again attain clarity and become honest with yourself and with your fellow people.

People who speak differently than they feel and think are dishonest. They can become hypocritical, deceitful or even wrong. Certainly, you don't want to be dishonest or false. For this reason, strive to be honest with your fellow people.

God, our heavenly Father, shows you each day what you should clear up.

He also shows you this in conversations with teachers, schoolmates, parents, brothers and sisters and through all the other people you meet and those to whom your attention is drawn via your senses.

In the evening, the players then report how it went, what the day brought to them, how their reactions to conversations were, what they felt, thought and spoke and what they overcame and in what way.

Dear brother, dear sister, in overcoming your human faults and weaknesses, you are not alone, for Christ, your Redeemer, the helping Spirit who dwells in you, supports and helps you to recognize yourself and to overcome with His power what is human and what you are able to overcome today with it.

If you have cleared up what you have recognized and have surrendered it to Christ, the redeeming Spirit in you, or you have spoken to the person to whom you said ugly or hateful things, and if you have asked for forgiveness, then examine how it went for you afterward and what you felt or still feel in yourself. Talk this over with your fellow players, because everyone can learn from everyone else.

Dear parents, strive to encourage such and similar games again and again. Set aside one or more days when you will play these games of insight with your children. And don't forget to sit together again in the late afternoon or evening and to report what the day of insight has brought, and how the players were able to master it or what their failure consisted of.

If parents are not shy of openly showing their children their good and less-good sides, then the children will also do this. This then results in a true understanding between parents and children.

Such group games are an enrichment in life and, in time, form a fraternal bond between parents and children. This fraternal bond lasts through the years of adolescence and beyond, when the children are adults and have children themselves.

This bond of love and tolerance, of honesty and freedom connects parents and children. It can last a whole lifetime on Earth – and beyond that, as selfless love in eternity.

I may repeat: These games of insight are an enrichment for all players, for the adults as well as for the children and young people.

I would like to now go back to the children between six and nine years of age.

Dear sister, dear brother, you have already gone through many schooldays or a couple of years of school. You had to experience that no day is like another. Just as the weather changes constantly and can be very different, so can it also be with the fluctuations of people's disposition.

Your disposition also fluctuates.

You, too, have a different mood each day: one day you are cheerful and happy, another time anxious and despondent or sad.

The various occurrences in the day determine your disposition and your daily rhythm.

The daily occurrences give the impulses for your conscious mind and subconscious and for the shadowed or light-filled sides of your soul. They give you the impetus to think about yourself: What can I do better today than during the past recent days?

They also remind you of what you have already overcome and are thus finished with. These are joyful realizations.

Each day serves each person and wants to stimulate them to self-recognition. Thus, the energies of the day touch the disposition of each person. They give them the possibility to recognize their sunny and shadowed sides. They should rejoice about their sunny sides. They should also thankfully accept the shadowed sides; because they can clear up what the day brings them, which makes this possible for them.

The fluctuations of your disposition will continue to exist until your soul has become light-filled and your conscious mind and subconscious have become clear. Only then, can you be balanced each day and stand above the moods and inhibitions of your neighbor. Note well, you stand above them, but you don't put yourself above your neighbor!

It is the goal of every soul in a human being to be free, happy and close to God. Someone who always reacts in a balanced and selfless way, who, out of selflessness, is loving in their feelings, thoughts, words and deeds, is very close to the divine, to the power of love of our heavenly Father. Such people meet their fellow people selflessly, kindly and tolerantly.

Perhaps you again have the concentrated lesson hours in school behind you. Were you always attentive? Did you always listen and participate? Were you understanding toward your schoolmates?

Tell whatever you have on your mind to your parents. You should also tell your teddy, doll, cat or other favorite playmate about what is going on inside you.

Once you have expressed this, then you are relaxed and free and can hear a true story by your sister Liobani, or even read one yourself.

Liobani Continues to Narrate

The elemental spirits

Dear sister, dear brother, I'll now tell you about the activity of the nature beings that you call gnomes, dwarfs and elves. I will tell you where they live and how they communicate with one another and with all other life forms.

You have already heard that the elemental or nature beings live and work on reserves. Many nature beings are on a reserve that corresponds to their spiritual level of development and to their spiritual capabilities. The reserves are large regions or territories.

Thus, the elemental spirits of the air, that is, the air spirits, have their regions and territories where they are active.

An air-region can be over a big city or a country, for example; it can even extend over a whole continent. The same applies for the fire and water spirits.

The earth spirits and the mountain spirits, which you will hear about later, are likewise assigned to certain reserves or regions.

You will perhaps ask who assigns the elemental beings to the reserves.

It is the eternal cosmic law, the heavenly Order.

You have heard that according to the cosmic law, like attracts like. According to this, the distribution into the reserves takes place automatically.

As with all other elemental spirits, there are also earth spirits on various levels of development. According to their state of consciousness, an elemental being is attracted to a reserve that has the same vibration as its consciousness. There, it then carries out its service to the life forms.

Consciousness means becoming aware. This applies to the elemental beings as well as to the souls of human beings.

The spiritual consciousness of people corresponds to what they – in their soul – have again opened from the eternal truth.

When people put good, selfless thoughts into practice, that is, when they actualize them, then their soul, and with that, their consciousness, becomes more light-filled and alert. As a result, the person lives more consciously; they know why they think this and achieve that.

Whatever an elemental being becomes aware of – that is, what has awakened in and on it – is the divine law. The elemental beings apply this in their reserves. Thus, they fulfill the eternal law in the air as well as in fire, in the light, in water and in and on the Earth.

The earth spirits, the gnomes, dwarfs and elves are the elemental beings that have matured the most.

In their development, these advanced nature beings resemble small children. Their faces and their forms are, however, not so finely shaped as those of a human child. Their appearance is still bizarre, this means that it doesn't yet have the fully developed form like that of a nicer human body.

First, I would like to report about the soil spirits. They are a developmental level of the earth-spirits.

These nature beings are responsible for the soil and for farmland. They look like an upright and well-formed clod of soil. In contrast to all other earth spirits, the soil spirits still have a bent body; their legs are too short and their arms too long. Their head has no real form, and is usually wider than it is high. Their body's radiation is darker than that of the earth spirits that work in the woods and in people's gardens.

All elemental beings are in harmony among themselves. Their tasks in gardens, woods, wetlands and meadows are coordinated with one another, so that, together, they form a great helping service, which has an effect on all spheres of life, in the air, in fire and water, in and on the Earth.

The elemental spirits are led by spirit beings that you call angels. These instruct them in God's laws again and again and support them when people's misbehavior causes things to happen – in the air, in water, with fire, in and on the Earth, and with which the elemental spirits don't know how they should act. Therefore, there are innumerable angel beings placed over the elemental spirits. They serve as teachers, guards and protectors of the elemental spirits. They also work on the reserves according to their mentality and their capabilities, helping and serving the elemental spirits.

Dear little brother or sister, understand that everything is well-ordered in all of infinity and that the divine hierarchy of love and service extends over matter – the coarsest structure in the universe.

There is no here and there. The divine world is everywhere. The one who is of pure heart can see and hear it.

Now I come back to the soil spirits.

The soil spirits live underground, usually in invisible caves.

As with all other elemental spirits, male and female principles exist with them, too. You people would say that they are of the male or female gender. In the spiritual world, however, there are no genders, but rather principles, that is, the imprinting of a man and a woman.

Genders exist only on Earth in the material forms, in human beings and animals, because the earthly garment, the physical body, has to be procreated by a physical body. In the spiritual world and thus, also among the elemental beings, man and woman live together, that is, two principles, the male and the female.

However, these pairs don't live alone and separated from similar entities. Together with several pairs of brothers and sisters, they form a large community.

Surely you would now like to know if they also have children. Well, that is a completely different story. Nature beings do not have children in the same way that people do, where a man lets the life for the child flow into the woman's body, so that an egg cell divides in the woman's body and from this, a human body then grows.

You know that in every human body a soul, a spirit body, is incarnated; that means that a spirit body gradually slips into the human shell.

The elemental beings don't have a material body, but a spirit body that is still in the process of spiritual development. Thus, the pairs, the elemental beings, are also in spiritual development.

You now ask whether the nature beings have children. The pairs of nature beings receive from the heavenly developmental planes nature beings which are not quite as developed as themselves – the woman and the man – which, for example, are still soil spirits.

Thus, when nature spirits that have become a pair develop to the next higher nature form and are at the end of this degree of maturity – which takes a very long time in human terms – then, to this pair, for example, to the soil pair, come one or several nature beings from the spiritual development planes of heaven, which are then taken in by this pair as their "sibling children." The parents, for instance, the soil beings or soil spirits, then help their sibling children to experience and to actualize what they, the soil pair, have already fulfilled.

When the nature beings come to the Earth from the heavenly development planes, then they are accompanied by angels that preside over the respective reserves from which the nature beings are attracted from the eternal homeland. At the same time, nature beings go from the Earth back to the spiritual development planes of the heavens, in order to continue their development there. They are the elemental beings that change over to a higher form of their genus in the heavens.

Therefore, this change of the nature beings to the next higher form does not take place on matter, on the Earth, but in the fine, subtle, divine vibrations of the eternal kingdom of light.

Dear brother, dear sister, you should also learn that no spirit form sleeps. Only human beings and animals on Earth need sleep.

All nature forms like flowers, bushes and trees have periods of rest.

Think of the seasons: spring, summer, autumn and winter. The trees and bushes, flowers and plants that have shown themselves in their splendor and abundance in spring rest throughout the winter. In autumn, the life, which stimulated growth, slowly withdraws. This often lasts into the winter.

In the autumn and winter, in this phase of rest, these life forms prepare themselves again for spring, for further growth.

All spiritual life forms in the kingdom of the eternal Being, the spirit beings and elemental beings, the spiritual life forms of animals and plants, merely rest; they do not sleep.

To rest means: The spirit body is not active – for the Spirit, the flowing energy that permeates everything, including the resting spirit body, is awake. The life energy in the resting spirit body registers everything that is important, so that – if necessary – it can give the right impulses, that is, to help or to give strength through an increased outflow of energy.

This is how the nature beings, for example, the soil beings, the elves, gnomes, imps or dwarfs rest in their homes.

There are so-called resting benches there. These are beautiful, well-formed stones that serve the nature beings as resting places. Often, these stones are covered with a slippery fluid, with moist earth, you would say, with a gelatinous mass. Like all the nature beings, the soil beings along with other soil pairs and their sibling children form a large family.

When the evolutionary path of a nature being that is developing via the animal kingdom has ended, then it gradually receives the form of a mature nature being.

As soon as a form changes from animal to nature being the characteristic of serving begins to take shape more distinctly. Thus, the life as nature beings is given in order to learn to serve.

The nature beings have come from the spiritual kingdom into the condensed zones, onto matter, that is, onto the Earth, to serve those life forms there that are developing. According to their developed consciousness, they serve and help all those life forms that are able to perceive them. The soil beings help, for example, the innumerable tiny animals that I also call the nature or earth cleaners. These are the many tiny animals and microorganisms that live and work in the soil, that aerate the soil and enrich and nourish it with their life; surely you know the moles, mice and earthworms. There are, however, still many other tinier animals.

Wherever these earth animals, the small animals and microorganisms are lacking, the soil is acidic, hard and in time infertile.

Now I come back to the soil beings.

They are also in harmony with all other elemental beings. The fire, water, air and earth spirits constitute a great helping community. Each call on the other for help, for each one has different capabilities and qualities.

For example, the soil spirits call either the fire, water, air or further developed earth spirits when it concerns helping and serving the earth animals. The soil spirits help a lot with their state of consciousness. When, for instance, a microorganism is in danger of suffocating or a small animal is drowning, then they call the air and water spirits to help. These nature helpers are immediately on site, and help the earth animals that are in danger, as far as it is possible for them.

For example, the air spirit tries to help a small, weak earth animal that is having difficulty breathing, perhaps a mouse, by increasing the element air and blowing it to the earth animal, so that it can breathe in more life force, and is again able to breathe deeply and receive the strength to find its way out of a possible danger zone.

If a small earth animal is in danger of drowning because of flooding, for example, then the soil spirits call the water and air spirit for help. They help the small animal. The water spirit stimulates the wave activity and the air spirit pushes the waves, that is, the water, away from the small animal. Either it then again feels land under its feet or it gains so much strength that it can find its way out of the danger zone. The soil spirits then receive it and warm its body, by directing healing and warming rays, which flow out of their spirit body, to the weakened small animal. The children of the soil spirits, which, of course, also want to help, then accompany the rescued little mouse into its earthly home or into a nearby home of a similar earth animal. The weak little animal can then recover there.

The soil beings also have the task to serve the spirit radiation of the microorganisms and small animals when they leave their little earthly bodies, that is, when their bodies, the material forms, die.

All nature beings, the soil beings, the forest, field and garden beings, the elves, gnomes and the elemental forms of the air, fire and water spirits as well, are, figuratively speaking, also spiritual midwives. They help the dying animals in the water, on and in the soil and in the air, so that the life-rays of the microorganisms and small animals and of the part-souls of the further developed animal species leave their earthly body without great difficulty. The same applies to the life-rays in flowers, plants, bushes and trees.

And so, you see, dear child, that the divine world lives among human beings, animals and plants, and is unceasingly ready to serve and to help human beings, animals, plants and also stones.

The forest spirits

Dear little sister, dear little brother, I would now like to tell you about the further developed nature beings, about the forest spirits, which human beings call imps or dwarfs. How do they live and what are they there for?

The forest spirits live under old gnarled trees that have a maze of roots. In such a maze of roots, hollow spaces often develop that one could also call small caves. Through their spirit power, the dwarfs expand these hollow spaces into beautiful, spacious, spiritual apartments.

The further developed forest spirits, also called nature spirits, also live in large families. Here, too, many families make up a great work of serving.

I repeat for your better understanding.

The male nature beings are called imps or dwarfs by human beings. The female nature beings are called elves. Man and woman, the dwarf and the elf, and also their sibling children live in peace with one another. As with the soil spirits, the sibling children find their way from the spiritual development spheres into their families through attraction.

Together, they help and serve the less developed life forms, the flowers, bushes and animals.

The forest spirits, like all other elemental spirits, also live on reserves, that is, in certain regions, in which they fulfill their tasks for plants and animals.

There are also resting and sitting benches in the living quarters of the forest beings. They are made out of beautifully curved roots.

When night covers a continent, the forest spirits go to their living quarters. They meet in their common rooms and lie down on their small root benches. They report about the day's occurrences, about their activities as invisible helpers and servers of nature and of the animal world. They also report about their encounters with human beings and tell about how they were able to help them.

Elf "Faith Little" reports

The elf, Faith Little, tells of her service, and how she was able to show the way again to someone who lost their way in the forest, and how the helping impulses that she emitted flowed into the person's memory. The person suddenly remembered where they came from and then knew to where they had to direct their steps to come out of the forest and find their way again.

Dear child, you should know that just as the guardian angels know how to lead people via their world of sensations and senses, so do the elemental beings know how to affect people's world of sensations and senses, without influencing their free will.

The elf reports. "Lost in thought, the man took one time this path and then another path in the woods, without paying attention to the trail signs that people put up for orientation. Thus, the man even left the path and went straight through the woods and through a thicket. Just as his thoughts had strayed, so did he also stray and lose his way. He saw neither the woods nor the thicket, and didn't even notice that he had left the path. He walked and walked and walked.

I tried," thus spoke the elf Faith Little, "to have an effect on him with my sensations, so as to help him. But this was not possible for me alone. And so, I called an air spirit and a fire spirit for help. But even they couldn't get through to the hiker. The man became more and more immersed in his world of thoughts and in his fate.

We elemental spirits had to let him keep on walking. But we stayed at his side; we accompanied him. At the same time, as impulses of awakening and help, we sent sensations of love. The hiker got tired and lay down on the woods' floor and fell fast asleep.

Now, a new possibility to help was given to me. I called the shore flies and instructed them about their task. With their soft humming and with the beating of their wings, it is possible for them to calm a person's restless aura and to magnetize certain energy-poor areas of the body – or also to relax tense spots, so-called energy knots. When the flies move in the aura of a sleeping person, they activate this magnetic field."

If the flies land on the body of the person, and then tickle these places, then the flies, the nature helpers, are trying to relax the tense nerves. It is usually very annoying to a person, because it tickles and makes them nervous. But in reality, such flies are trying to help the person!

You know, dear child, that like always attracts like. When certain types of flies are foreseen for these and similar purposes, that is, to magnetize and relax the human energy field, the aura, and the atmosphere, then this is their task for human beings, animals and nature, and they take their task seriously. In most cases, however, this is irritating for the person, because they feel disturbed by the flies. Actually, the person's nervous system is disturbed, that is, tense, and the aura is also restless. That means that the magnetic field, the person's aura, is in disharmony.

Thus, the flies buzz around sleepers and penetrate ever deeper into their aura, into their magnetic surroundings, until they have reached the body. They light on those places that are very tense.

The unpleasant irritation made by the flies makes the person do movements that normally would not be made, for example: The person hits out at the flies, slaps the arm, to drive the flies away or kill them. But the flies purposely trigger this reaction in the person, so that – in our case – the hiker or sleeper touches his tense body part more strongly. The result is that possible tensions or cramps there loosen up; the blood circulation increases, thus causing the brain cells to be supplied better with blood, so that now, by way of the person's world of sensations, the impulses of help from the nature beings reach the person's world of thoughts.

When you hear about shore flies, these are certain kinds of flies that don't bite. They have the task of bringing relaxation into the atmosphere, into nature, into people and animals, that is, to relieve tension.

And so, the flies' activity can also bring about a real relaxation in a person, so that the person is again receptive to positive, hopeful thoughts.

"So the shore flies began their work," reported the elf. "It took a long time until our hiker, who had fallen asleep, woke up again and finally got up. Before he woke up, he kept slapping himself more or less hard on his arm or foot, scratched his head or shook his whole body, to drive away the bothersome flies. Now, he was totally awake, and looked around thinking: 'Where am I?'

I perceived this question to himself and made contact again. By way of his memory, that is, his world of sensations and senses, I showed him how he could find his way out of his bewilderment and recognize the way home.

So, via his memory world I stimulated his sense of sight and, at the same time, awoke further memories that gave him the assurance that he was reacting cor-

rectly, as he found his way out of the confusion of his human ego, in order to reach the path that led him homeward.

I was very happy when the hiker got up, stretched himself, looked at his watch, shook his head and said to himself: 'Well, it's high time I went home. I really slept deeply!'

He also thought: 'It was certainly good for me, because now, I see things more clearly. I now know the solution to the problem that upset me so much.'

He looked around and again said to himself: 'Ah, here's a path. I'll look for a trail sign and then I'll find my way out!'"

"Dear brothers and sisters," the elf then said to all the listening nature beings, "you can well imagine how very much the shore flies and I rejoiced that we could help!

The shore flies and I accompanied him for part of the way, and then we suddenly saw his guardian angel, who waved lovingly to us. We now knew: The hiker is in good hands."

Dear human brothers and sisters, you should know that if people are very upset and harbor dark, brooding thoughts and nurture them, by pitying themselves, then the guardian spirit has to keep a greater distance from their charge, because the person's aura is very restless and sparks of anger or hate are being sent out.

The possibility of help, however, is manifold. Nature beings, air, fire and water spirits and many other positive forces are helpers for the material forms, for people, animals, plants and minerals.

When the elf had finished her report, the elder of the large family, "Mr. Rootman," a wise, that is, already more matured, forest spirit, spoke great praise to the little, delicate elf. He asked her to invite the industrious shore flies for the next evening, when that part of the Earth turns away from the sun and the forest and meadow spirits carry out their sun dance, a prayer of thanks to the All-Spirit.

The elf was glad and sent out the invitation right away via waves of sensations. The shore flies answered via waves of sensations and gave thanks for the invitation, which, of course, they gladly accepted.

Sly Fox

Encouraged by Little Trusting elf's story, a forest being that was already one of the mature nature beings began to report.

It said: "Dear elves you have encouraged me to also contribute to the joy. This morning I went through the woods to see that everything was in order.

I went through our reserve and checked in at the homes of the deer, hares, foxes and squirrels to see if everything was in order.

In the number two den, by family Sly Fox, a very subdued atmosphere prevailed. Father Fox, who had to feed his hungry children, had not returned home from his foray through the woods and fields. Where could he be?

Mrs. Fox said: 'He went far away. As he was underway, I received the signal from him that he wanted to go to the next village to get the fox children something special to eat.

That was his last sign of life.'

I know my duty, for I'm on this reserve to help. I asked myself: 'What can be done when the village is outside of my reserve?'

I promised to help. Then I went all the way to the edge of our reserve. From there I saw the village lying in the morning dawn."

Dear human children, you should know that nature beings also exist that are responsible for the lives of animals, plants and stones in the villages, towns and even cities. These nature beings are those that are the most developed, many of whom have already reached the preliminary stage of the filiation of God.

The forest being continued:
"I now sent out sensations and energies to the village. I called the elder of the nature beings who is responsible for the spiritual care of the village and the surrounding area.

He, himself, did not respond, but his wife, elf "Accept Me", did. She promised to do all in her power to find Mr. Sly Fox.

From the border of our reserve, I briefly sent out my sense of sight and spotted several nature beings that were swiftly seeking Mr. Sly Fox.

Soon after, Mr. Accept Me, the elder of the nature spirits in the village, signaled via his sensations that Mr. Sly Fox had been found.

Mr. Sly Fox howled pitifully from inside a tightly closed barn. He had wanted to hide in there until it was time for him go after his prey. However, the owner of the barn had shut the door and Mr. Sly Fox was trapped.

And this is the way the nature beings freed him:

Invisible as they are for humans, they went into the house of the barn's owner. He was just stretching in his bed and preparing to get up. The elder of the nature spirits sent impulses into the owner's sensory world that he should open the barn door, because the sun and air would be good for the damp stone walls. And at best, he should open both barn doors so that lots of air and sun would dry the walls.

The barn's owner took in these impulses. He thought: 'The first thing I'll do is open the barn doors. Besides that, I then have to drive the tractor in there to the repair shop.'

He got up, washed and dressed himself. Before he had breakfast, he went to the barn, opened both doors, drove the tractor outside and went back in the house. Like a flash of lightning, Mr. Sly Fox bolted out and ran past the nature spirits of the village – without even taking notice of them or thanking them. He made a beeline for the reserve where he and his family lived.

I stood in his pathway to stop Mr. Sly Fox, who was totally agitated. He paused, panting. He was breathing very rapidly and his heart raced with fear.

I said: 'Now, Mr. Sly Fox, you don't want to bring disgrace to your name and destroy thriving life, do you? There's plenty of carrion for you in nature. Besides that, think of your spiritual origin and change the cravings of your senses. May this fateful lesson show you that nature provides for all of us, including your family. Take gratefully from nature what it gives you today and feed your children honestly.

I am going to your family now and report that you're coming home. And for your family, now go look to see what nature has provided for you today.'

Mr. Sly Fox put his bushy tail between his legs and crept away.

Via my powers of sensation, I thanked the nature beings of the village, especially Mr. Accept Me, who had organized the search and rescue effort."

The elder of the large family of nature beings, Mr. Rootman, said: "You should invite our nature brothers and sisters, the nature beings of the village, to a prayer dance at sunset with us."

And that's how it happened.

The little fawn

Encouraged by the stories of the forest beings and filled with joy that they are also nature helpers, the little elf Go-with-Me raised its soft voice and said:

"I, too, experienced something nice as I went hand-in-hand through the woods with our neighbor's son 'Hannilove.' In the morning, we also walked through the reserve to visit a few animal families. As we went calmly and attentively on our way, we sent out our fine sensations, in order to sense where help was needed. We then heard plaintive cries in the distance.

We followed our senses and could hear the plaintive cries coming from a thicket. The little fawn, 'Mother Love', lay there in pain crying pitifully. We said to it, dear little fawn, Mother Love, we bring you the sun's greetings. What happened? We understood from the little fawn's sensations that early in the morning it was grazing. Suddenly it heard shots.

Still so awkward as it is, it wanted to flee over stones and rough terrain back to its mother. But the fawn hit its foot against a rock so that it was now hurting badly.

Hannilove took a closer look at the leg and concluded that it was broken. 'What shall we do now?' asked Hannilove. 'Such a broken leg has to be bandaged, if not even splinted. From the sunrays, we could reinforce the soothing and healing forces and direct them to Mother

Love; but we need the help of a human being to set the broken bone.

'What can we do?' I said to Hannilove.

Hannilove thought and said: 'I received the solution.

A forest ranger often goes through this area. We know that he loves animals and that he has often helped animals. He always carries along a tube.'

By that, Hannilove meant to say a strong bandage. He often used this on animals, especially deer, to bandage a leg.

'But so early in the morning he's not yet underway. That's why we want to absorb the first rays of sun into our hands. With our love sensations for the Creator-Spirit, we'll reinforce the sun's rays in our hands and transmit these to Mother Love, to ease the pain.'

So that's how it happened:

The little elf, Go-with-Me and the gnome, Hannilove, held open their hands to absorb the first rays of the sun.

They prayed to the Creator-God for strength and help for the little fawn, Mother Love. They directed the healing rays to the little fawn's body.

"Soon after that," continued the little elf, Go-with-Me, "the little fawn's big eyes were shining again. The worse pain was over.

Now Hannilove said, 'Little elf, you stay with Mother Love and I will go to find the friendly forest ranger.'

Hannilove called a fire spirit for help and said:

'Together we will direct the forest ranger to Mother Love.' Hannilove petted the little fawn and also stroked my hair lovingly and said: 'You can count on me, dear little elf.'

My heart overflowed and I said: 'I know, Hannilove, you will bring help.'"

Hannilove then went out of the thicket.

The sun's radiance of the young morning shone in his heart. He didn't need to think about where he should now go and look.

You should know, dear human child, that when a heart is filled with love, then beings and people are guided by the power of love, and they experience much that is wonderful and good.

Hannilove heard the fire spirit in his heart:

"Hannilove, I received your call for help. In front of you a sunray is flashing in a flower. It shines in your heart."

Hannilove saw the flower in front of him and, at the same time, sensed in his heart that the flower was showing the way on which he would meet the forest ranger. As Hannilove looked at the flower, it nodded its head. Now Hannilove knew the direction that he had to take.

An air spirit also had come to help him and had blown on the flower, so that its little head pointed in the direction that Hannilove had to take.

Again and again, on his way, he met the same type of flower. The flower nodded with its head again and again and showed him the way.

It was, of course, the air spirit that showed Hannilove the way to the forest ranger, via the flower children.

Suddenly Hannilove stopped.

He heard heavy steps; the forest floor vibrated. It was the forest ranger!

Now what was needed was to direct the good man, who strolled along in thought, to the underbrush where the fawn Mother Love lay.

As long as the forest ranger took the right way to the thicket everything was good.

Gnome Hannilove went along next to him, very little in comparison to the big person. But Hannilove's heart was full of love and his being had inner greatness, the selflessness to help where help was needed.

The forest ranger stopped and set off in another direction.

Hannilove directed his heart sensations to the forest ranger's senses, but he did not react to this.

Hannilove then called the fire spirit.

"I am already here," he said and caused a sunray to flash very brightly on the ranger's left.

Surprised, the forest ranger looked to the left and went on.

Hannilove sent another helping impulse, which stimulated him to go and see if everything was in order. At the same time, the fire spirit intensified a sun's ray that landed on a splinter of glass, which flashed and began to sparkle.

The forest ranger said to himself: "Oops, now I must see what's lying there! It could start a forest fire."

He turned around and went the way that led to the underbrush. He found the glass splinter, picked it up, put it in his pocket and went on.

While Hannilove was on the way to get help, little elf Go-with-Me stayed with the little fawn, Mother Love. She also sent out sensations of peace and calmness to the fawn's mother.

Mother Love felt pain again and again.

When a stronger wave of pain came, the little fawn gave out a loud cry. This happened just as the forest ranger wanted to pass by the thicket.

He stopped: "What was that? That was the cry of a deer," he thought. "It must be very nearby. Something is moving over there."

Mother Love heard the forest ranger and wanted to get up and run away but it collapsed. It could not stand. Frightened and with a pounding heart, it just lay there, while the ranger crept through the underbrush and carefully came closer.

The ranger's kind heart was moved when he saw the beautiful fawn lying there. He spoke consoling words to it and very cautiously approached the fawn, which was becoming ever more uneasy, but couldn't stand up.

The ranger recognized the fawn's situation very quickly. He took the so-called "tube" out of his pocket, about which Hannilove has spoken, the strong bandage; then he looked for appropriate small pieces of wood to stabilize the leg. And he found them, because the elf and gnome helped as much as they could.

The ranger splinted the leg and firmly wrapped the "tube" around it. The fawn didn't like this, but little elf Go-with-Me and gnome Hannilove explained everything to it. Then it kept still.

When the leg was splinted and bandaged, the ranger lifted up fawn Mother Love, but it still couldn't stand on its own. It collapsed and lay on the twigs again, which were already pressed down like a sleeping hollow. The ranger examined his efforts to see if it would hold firmly. He stroked the fawn's coat and softly murmured to it: "Stay lying here, nothing can happen to you. There are no foxes around here. I'll visit you again in the evening. If you're still here then, I'll take you to my forest cabin." He left.

The little elf continued:

"Hannilove and I intensified the sun's rays over and over again and directed the healing forces to the broken leg. At the same time, we sent out sensations of love, sensations that signaled help. In this way, via an air spirit and a fire spirit, the fawn's mother could be reached; she had already been looking for her child. The air spirit and the fire spirit guided the mother deer to the thicket where she found her fawn. She comforted it and lay down next to it. She licked it with her tongue, and stroked her tongue over its back, lovingly licked its ears, thus giving it love and security.

You should know, dear human child, that the sensations of selfless love are the language of animals, plants, stones and elemental beings. All spiritual life forms are connected with one another by selfless sensations of love.

In this way, the doe lovingly cared for her child for several hours; then she got up and showed her child that it should get up and go with her. Mother Love wanted to get up, but it collapsed over and over again. The doe lovingly went back to Mother Love again and again and sent it sensations that said: "support yourself on three legs and balance yourself with the fourth."

After several attempts, the fawn stood and limped after its caring mother, who brought it to safety in the camp of the deer family, called Jump-in-the-Field, to which Mother Love belonged. It is hidden in a large thicket under a tree. Its branches hang protectively over the hollow, on which much grass and leaves lie.

Hannilove and I accompanied the doe and her fawn. In their camp was another fawn that was very happy that Mother Love was back again. It made room and warmed

Mother Love with its body. The joy in the deer camp was great because Mother Love had been found again and the mother then stayed with the children and protected them."

Dear human child, it is similar with you human beings as well:

Whoever is kind and loving to their neighbor, who thinks and loves selflessly, receives a lot of joy and love. You should know that selfless love, which flows into the heart of your neighbor, causes a mighty force, out of which love flows, in turn – which heals where healing is necessary, which helps where help is needed and which unifies those who long for unity.

Dear human brothers and sisters, see, in this way the elemental spirits help the animals and the plants that have an earthly garment.

The nature spirits also strive to help human beings, if they are able to reach the people's world of sensations with their sensations of love.

Robin Redbreast

The gnome, Hannilove and the elf, Go-with-Me continued their story: "This task was completed. Soon we saw our next task.

This morning had already determined our daily plan. It was under the motto, 'help through people.' We then went through the forest to visit the elf family, 'Flowers Fine.'"

You should know, dear human child, that there are also nature beings whose task it is to be responsible for the various kinds of flowers.

"As we went through the forest," reported the elf, "to visit the family Flowers Fine on the meadow, who were already very busy at work, we heard strange sounds.

'That must be a bird,' said Hannilove.

We sent out our sensations and registered within us that near the wood glade a robin sat with its wing hanging limply down.

We went toward the glade and saw the robin called 'Swing-Along.' It hopped here and there on the floor of the woods, jumping from one tree root to another.

We saw that it could no longer fly.

What had happened?

Hannilove said: 'The pain is worse than the cause. But this is again a task for a kind person, a nature friend, because purely material help is needed.'

The young robins were crying in the tree and wanted to be fed. What could be done?

We communicated from within with the robin Swing-Along and perceived that – frightened by a shot – it had injured its bone with its beak, and wanting to quickly fly away, had, with its reaction, dislocated its wing.

'I can already lift it,' said robin Swing-Along, 'but I'm in a lot of pain.'

'So again, it was a shot,' said Hannilove, 'which the fawn Mother-Love mentioned.' Is there a poacher on our reserve that's after prey? If this is the case, then there will be more suffering. – But now, we want to help 'Swing-Along.'

The sun was already high in the sky. Hannilove and I held up our hands to intensify the sun's rays and transmit them to the little bird.

But robin Swing-Along was anxious and could therefore absorb only little of the soothing and healing power of the sun – for the hungry children were crying pathetically up in the tree.

May it be said to you, dear human children:

Despite all difficulties, always strive to stay calm. Then help can be granted to you in manifold ways. Every anxiety creates new disquiet and tenses the nerves. Disquiet also increases the fearfulness.

This was not the case with the robin. It was worried about its hungry babies.

Hannilove said to me: "Elf Go-with-Me, you stay with Swing-Along. I'll go look for a human being who can help here.

So, I stayed with the robin.

Hannilove disappeared and right after that, some children arrived. They were walking at the edge of the woods and talking together.

'Be quiet,' said one of the children, I hear cheeping. That must be a bird.'

It was the little bird Swing-Along.

The children crept carefully forward and discovered the crying robin.

One of the children said:

'Stand here quietly. I'll catch the robin and take it home.' The child cautiously approached the robin. But it was frightened and because of this, it didn't think of the pain.

It just had the feeling it should fly away.

And it made exactly the movements that were needed to reset its wing.

The wing went back in place and Swing-Along flew crying to a nearby branch, on which it was safe from the children. It stayed perched on the branch – of course, with its heart beating wildly. It still felt a dull pain, but the wing was again able to fly.

When the children had left, I encouraged the robin to see to its young. And Swing-Along then did that.

Dear human children, people can help in such a way, consciously and also unconsciously.

You have now heard that animals, plants and stones have feelings. The nature and mineral kingdoms take in the selfless, loving sensations of people as well as their unpleasant sensations, feelings and thoughts.

If the people are loving and kind, then the nature and mineral kingdoms radiate their harmonious powers to them. However, if people are angry and brutal, by killing animals for pleasure, by deliberately pulling up plants and flowers and cutting down trees filled with sap, or breaking up stones with huge machines or forcibly moving masses of earth, then the life forms withdraw their powers and remain closed off, that is, they do not radiate any life force to the negative people.

"When Hannilove returned without success, the little bird Swing-Along was already looking for food. But he had received my waves of sensations and knew that the robin was already feeling well again.

Hannilove and I went over the meadows and sat down in the midst of the flowers.

We let ourselves be fanned by the moving grass and absorbed the fragrance of the flowers.

We talked about our experiences and that several unpleasant occurrences must have occurred in the reserve, because certainly many animals had heard the shots.

The family Flowers Fine saw us sitting in the meadow and came to us. We reported our experiences and were glad that we were able to help as much as we could.

The family Flowers Fine told us that early in the morning an angry person had hastily run over the meadow toward the village. He carried a rifle in his hand, but had no prey. We were all very glad about this and thanked the Creator-God.

Via waves of sensations, we informed all the helpers in the reserve, the elves and gnomes, about our experiences, and that the man, who was perhaps a poacher, had run back to the village without prey. The elves and gnomes confirmed that they had understood us.

Then together, all the nature beings sent out sensations of peace over the reserve.

The air spirits reinforced these waves of sensations. Thus, all the animals and life forms of nature could continue to emit their sensations of harmony."

And that's how a day in the life of the nature beings goes, always under the motto of helping and serving.

But when evening comes and this part of the Earth gradually turns away from the sun, when the last rays of the sun gently and lightly fall over the meadow, then the elves and gnomes begin their sun prayer after a full day of work.

It is the sun dance, to which many guests are also invited. Together, all the nature beings worship the Creator-Spirit; He is the Spirit of evolution in them. He refines their structure and form and also their sensations more and more – until they have reached the filiation of God and have become images of the heavenly Father.

The Sun Dance –
A prayer dance of the nature spirits

The sun dance is the sun prayer of the nature spirits, that is, a prayer dance.

When the rays of the evening sun fall soft and golden on the large flowering meadows in the valleys, the nature beings, the gnomes and the elves of the woods, of the fields and meadows, of the cities, villages and towns, come together for the sun dance.

They join hands, that is, they put the left hand under the right hand, so that both hands form a bowl. In this bowl they absorb the light of the sun. They place their love in this bowl and radiate this love-light to the All-Spirit.

The radiating, cosmic light in their hands says that God is light, power, harmony and peace. God is energy, radiating infinity; He is active in all Being.

The nature beings form two circles, an outer and an inner circle. The outer circle is formed by the gnomes, the inner circle by the elves.

The elemental spirits are also there and each one carries a light. Now, the sun dance begins. The air spirits provide the music. They draw their energies over the fine blades of grass, which are shone upon by the sun. The fine large and small blades are the strings of nature's violin and are strung, according to their texture, by the fire spirit.

This is how it happens:

The blades of grass, which are needed by the air spirit to play music, are irradiated by the fire spirit, through which increased energy flows to the blades. The air spirit then moves over the large and small blades and plays beautiful tunes for the nature spirits. In this way, music is created for the sun dance. Human ears can hear these melodies only intuitively.

Those who have trained the inner sense of hearing, the soul's ear, which can perceive the fine cosmic tones, hear within the harmonious melodies that the air spirit plays for the sun dance, which is prayer of thanks to the All-Spirit. These melodies are similar to the heavenly music of the spheres. The nature beings dance and enjoy the heavenly melodies.

The invited guests, for example, the swamp flies, also tune in with the sun dance, as much as this is possible. They buzz to the tunes and dance above the nature beings' heads. Each elf and each gnome holds a sunlight in its hands. When the outer circle turns to the left, then the inner circle turns to the right. And then they switch around: The outer circle then turns to the right and the inner circle to the left.

After this lively dance, the nature beings go toward each other: The outer circle, the gnomes, move toward the inner circle, to the elves. They exchange their lights. This is a symbol and means that in the gnome is the same power as in the elf, and in the elf, the same power that is in the gnome. After this, they put the exchanged lights on their heads; each gnome takes the right hand of an elf with its right hand and they all dance together. After this, they hold both hands together and raise their hands, so that both can see one another as through a window. This means: I see you as you are and you see me as I am.

And now they change partners, and with the next partner, the same symbolic dance follows: I see you and you see me, in a light, the light of love.

After the symbolic dance, they take the lights down from their heads and look at each other through the light. This means: I see you in the light of God.

Afterward, they surrender their lights to the last rays of the sun with the request that their lights make all people meek, and may people find the inner light and may they live the selfless, serving love.

Lastly, the nature beings form a large circle. Between two gnomes there is one elf respectively. Together they swing and dance in a circle, first to the right and then to the left.

They sing many songs to the various melodies, which the air spirits play.

One of their many songs goes like this:

Dance, sing, swing and hum with us.
The Spirit rises from the meadow ground.
He joins in song with us.
Elves, gnomes, fire, air and water spirits
are united in eternal unity.
We sing the song to the One
who is the love Himself.

Nightingales, robins, sparrows
sing good night.
All animals of fields and forests
are united in chorus.
Every manifested pure spirit praises God's love.

All worlds are in you and are in me.
If you recognized yourself, then you recognize me.
I love you and you love me.
Look not here and there.
Look in yourself.
There you find your brother, your sister;
and you also find me,

the little elf, the gnome,
the little animal and the fine plant.
All feel each other and all are one.
We thank the great Creator-God.
We know no need.
Everything, everything is in us.
It is God, the very base.

Great Spirit,
the day is fading;
spiritual growth and maturing continue in us.
Every day is light.
It increases in elf, in gnome,
in the person, the animal, in all Being.
Great God, we thank You.
You are the light and we are in Your light.
We continue to mature
and You will continue to rise in us,
until we enter the filiation of God.
Then we are the images of Your creating power.

O All-Spirit,
that is, then, the Father-Mother-filiation.
Great Spirit,
in You, we see light in the day and night.
We take our rest;
the earthly night covers the day.
And yet, the night indicates the new morning,
for us to serve and help where we can.
The day awakens.
We praise You, O eternal light.

You give Yourself to me,
You give Yourself to all Being.
Life is eternity.

All creating powers that are present, the elves, the gnomes, the flower children, the animals in the water, on and in the soil and in the air, the fire and air spirits, all bow before the eternal power, the All-Spirit in every creature, in all Being. At the same time, they send out sensations of peace.

Peace streams over meadows, fields and woods, over villages, towns and cities.

Those who, as human beings, seek inner peace will find it in the evening atmosphere – if they take it in and feel as one with the stillness of nightfall. The night also has its song. Those who hear it have found their way into the stillness. The song of the stillness is like a prayer:

Peace, peace to all people.
Peace, peace to all souls.
Peace, peace into infinity.
Extend your arms,
and peace comes into your house and mine.
I keep peace with you,
then peace also stays in me.
Peace also in sleep.
Good night.

The elder of the large family community now rings a flower bell, which stands not far from their dwelling places.

As he rings, he praises the sibling children, the elves and the goblins and says:

"The peace of the night already bears within the new day.

Now we want to rest, so as to receive the new day in stillness and peace.

Have a good rest," says the elder and each of the family members seeks out their root, which serves them as a bench for resting.

However, the nature beings remain quite aware. This means that they don't sleep, but rest.

Their senses, however, remain awake and alert, so that they can notice, in good time, any dangers or other occurrences in the reserve, to then be able to work and help accordingly.

Dear human child, surely you had your thoughts as you listened to these true stories!

What touched you in a special way? And what did you think about?

Talk about this with your parents or with the person who shared this spiritual occurrence with you.

If you read it yourself, then you can tell your parents and your brothers and sisters about it and speak with them about it. It would be good if your mother or father could write down the acquired knowledge in your book of life. Your book of life could be called, for example, "Experiences of My Childhood" or "My Life's Experiences."

Dear child, if it is now time for you to sleep, so I wish you and your soul the peace and stillness of God – and a good journey for your soul, your spirit body; for your soul goes to that place where, according to its light-filled and shadowed sides, it is able to go, once your earthly body sleeps well and deeply. A light-filled, that is, a bright, soul goes to light-filled and beautiful worlds, which are far beyond the many Milky Ways.

A dark soul either remains on the Earth or goes – according to its light-poor condition – to those worlds where light-poor souls live.

Dear brother, dear sister, therefore, let your soul become filled with light. You have many possibilities to become and remain light-filled and strong. You can also read in this book how you become light-filled and how you remain light-filled and strong.

I wish your soul a light-filled journey and your body a healthy and deep sleep.

As you already know, your soul stays connected to your physical body by an energy cord, which is also called an information cord.

What the soul experiences flows through the information cord to your brain cells.

That is why it is possible that you experience in your dreams many things that are true, but only if your subconscious and your conscious mind are not filled with all-too-human things and your soul has become transparent for God's light.

Conversely, your physical body also communicates with the soul via the information cord. Via the information cord, your many nerves transmit to your travelling soul when you, the human being, go into a light sleep or when you wake up. Faster than you can think, your soul is back and is again in or around your body.

Your guardian spirit is the supervisor of these processes and monitors the travelling soul and your physical body. If, for example, you are startled by noises and wake up, or if danger threatens, then it calls your soul back in time; for the guardian spirit sees and recognizes the danger before it happens and it helps.

You also recognize by this that all of creation is based on selfless serving, on true love, which is divine love.

You should again become capable of this love.

On your way to selfless love, I may accompany you with my explanations from the divine kingdom, and show you how you should feel, think and live, so that you become divine again.

Good night, dear brother, dear sister.

Dear parents, time is moving on. In the meantime, your child has already had many experiences, both pleasant and unpleasant.

Dear parents, I, Liobani, wish from my heart that with my advice, I was able to give you help and support in many a case. With these words, I don't want to take my leave of you, but to conclude this part for the children between six and nine years of age.

For the Growing Youth from Nine to Twelve Years

For the parents

Dear parents, according to the eternal cosmic laws, your child is our brother or our sister, because the indwelling spirit being, the soul, is a child of God, like you, yourself. The child now comes into puberty.

The doll, the teddy bear and the cat or other favorite animals now become unimportant. They stand or sit in the cupboard or on a shelf and are allowed to go to sleep in the bed of the growing youth only now and then.

Reviewing the book of life

Dear parents, it would be the right time now to look back over the child's book of life.

Go through your child's book of life thoroughly and attentively. Which areas of their life went well and which not so well?

Also, look attentively at the drawings and pictures of the child as well as their handwriting.

Furthermore, you should also talk about the book of life with your child during a quiet hour, at best, toward evening when everything has calmed down outside and you, too, are mostly in harmony. The experiences that result from this can be guides for the child's further path through life.

Dear parents, please pay attention to your children's reactions as you go through the book of life with them.

When you come across critical parts, that is, those areas that are still unresolved by the child, which are set into motion by reading them, your child will become restless. Perhaps your child would like to say something but yet remains silent.

Such reactions indicate fear, inferiority complexes, failure or other difficulties. Be understanding with your children and cautiously ask them what they would like to say. Note down the important comments and whatever they answer to your understanding questions on a new page of the book of life, entitled: "Experiences with My Child," or "with My Son" or "with My Daughter."

Dear parents, if you frequently look at the book of life and speak about it with your growing child, you can recognize what is happening inside this growing adolescent. You sense the deep layers of their subconscious and understand what their joys or difficulties and problems want to tell you.

These are informative moments, in which you analyze the book of life; the growing youth will thereby become aware of many things, especially of what they have not yet overcome, what they still think about, that is, what preoccupies them. The writings and talks together call up in them what has accumulated in their subconscious – joy and sorrow, and the things overcome or that have not yet been overcome become evident.

With great understanding, you should accompany the transitional years from childhood, from six to nine years of age, to the years from nine to twelve. Dear parents, during this phase of life, it is your obligation of love to support your child or children with understanding, tolerance and good will.

This new phase in your child's life should also become evident in the book of life. Note on new pages of this book of insight whatever the child has overcome and what still has to be cleared up and overcome together.

Note the joys and also the past pains and sorrows of your child that possibly keep coming up in conversations with them. All these notes together enable a deep insight into the predispositions and inclinations of your child.

When there are still things to be cleared up and worked on, for example, misbehaviors that could lie many years in the past, or fears caused by the misconduct of parents or teachers, this should be cleared up during this phase as far as it is possible.

If your nine-year-old child still has an interest in the favorite animal or doll, then you, dear parents, can use this possibility to perhaps find out more by way of the doll, teddy or cat regarding what is still hidden in the subconscious, yet still active in the child.

When you thereby ask your child questions, as you did earlier, about what teddy, cat, doll or another favorite has to tell, and whether they think something still has to be cleared up soon, then wait and see if an answer doesn't come from the nine-year-old child.

Aptitude for a later occupation

Dear parents, when you question your nine to twelve-year-old child, please be cautious. They may not be pressing and controlling questions, but simple and clear questions, with which the children feel that they can decide for themselves which answers they would like to give. To the extent that a child still has a relationship to a favorite toy, teddy, doll or to the cat, then the question can be put in this way, for instance:

"Which occupation would the teddy, the doll or the cat suggest to you, because you will certainly want to practice an occupation after your school years?"

Unconsciously, many children think about what they will do one day. This already begins between the sixth and the ninth year of life. They indicate these conscious or unconscious sensations to their favorite animal, without thinking anymore about it.

The child experiences the father when he comes home from work. It is led by the mother's hand through stores where it sees sales persons, housewives and artisans. It experiences teachers, doctors, employees and other people in their occupational lives. The child unconsciously absorbs these activities and remarks. Unconsciously, the child tells its favorite toy which occupational wishes it has.

Dear parents, do not press your child with your questions and do not expect an answer immediately.

Self-reliance grows in a person, especially between the ages of nine and twelve. The youth would like to decide for themselves and not be pressured into a decision or having to fulfill expectations of parents. Young people have ideas that they would like to accomplish themselves.

If your child has already put away its favorite toy or speaks or plays with it only rarely, then you can ask your child directly, which occupation it would like to learn later on.

Especially when a change of schools is being considered, parents should know their child's inclinations, aptitudes and abilities.

Dear parents, please note the answers of your child or children in the book of life. It would certainly be good and informative to also talk with the teachers about your child's choice of an occupation, about the impressions they have of their pupil, as well as which capabilities and aptitudes they have recognized in this growing youth. These observations could also point to a continuing path of education. If your children attend a higher school of learning to be further trained in their capabilities, then make sure that this school also has workshops for manual trades where the young ones can possibly develop their other inclinations and capabilities.

The future schools in Universal Life should include the possibility to learn various occupations. There should be workshops integrated in the schools, in which the youth can develop their practical capabilities and talents. This will help their choice of an occupation.

During the first school years the children still learn in a playful manner. Here, the first indications already become evident regarding their predispositions, abilities, talents and inclinations. These show themselves even more clearly when they can carry out some small manual work.

If predispositions, inclinations, abilities and talents are encouraged early enough, then it can be recognized very soon for what the child is most suited, and it can then attend the secondary schools that correspond to its capabilities and foster them.

As I have already briefly mentioned, parents should not hinder the growing youth between nine and twelve in their urge for freedom, but they should speak and live with them in such a way that they feel that the parents are friends – and not dictators who want their will fulfilled by their child.

The growing youth

ear parents, the critical phase begins between the ninth and the twelfth years of life.

Then, the children begin to free themselves from their parents' supervision. This growing youth strives for self-reliance.

They should take their life into their own hands in succeeding years.

Dear parents, your child is growing up and does not want to be taken care of so much and protected as in childhood. The growing youth gradually recognize themselves. Their own desires and ideas are urging to be actualized.

In girls, as well as in boys, the hormones begin to work more strongly and press toward active sexuality. The young boy senses his manly power and the girl her development as a woman.

This transformation from a child to an adolescent and to adulthood has the effect that the present desires, longings and ideas that are in the soul gradually become more active.

The burdens of the soul also mature and radiate, via the genes and the person's senses, into the body. They direct the thinking, the wanting and the wishes and, at the same time, stimulate the person to self-recognition.

Young people gradually want to make decisions themselves. Often, they no longer want to be asked what they will do this afternoon. They no longer want to be patronized. They feel that they are no longer children. They think they know everything better and want to express their own feelings and sensations.

In this time of storm and stress, the growing youth no longer want to accept the viewpoints of older people. They have their own world view.

Anyone who wants to convince them otherwise will only increase this desire. The young person thinks that the advice and suggestions of fellow people may very well be good for them – but not for the young person.

During this critical time, the growing youth choose other friends and also look more closely when "the world" offers and presents its stimulations. The eruption of hormonal activity has an effect on young people's senses and particularly determines their life during this phase.

Dear parents, even if you have brought up your child in a free and selfless way according to the laws of love, despite everything, many parents now have to acknowledge that all this was of little avail. Your child, the growing youth, gets totally out of control. They no longer are the loving and understanding child that was so clever and wise between the ages of six and nine. They have turned into little savages and no longer want to be told anything by older persons, but listen more to young people who are perhaps a few years older – and are now their role model.

The young person now has other idols and ideals and perhaps imitates a star seen on television or someone met at youth gatherings.

What happened?

In the growing youth, it is not only the young person that is breaking out. The child is not only becoming a young person, but at the same time, the predispositions toward being a man and a woman are awakening in them.

The growing youth now no longer sees girls and boys – but two sexes. They recognize that man and woman have different characteristics, which the older people also call attractions. They become a more exacting observer. A young person is controlled further by their body's hormones and is led into the stage of life where they gradually recognize that their life is not only dependent on their parents, but also on their own thoughts and actions. Because of this development toward independence, ideas and desires emerge that are often contrary to those of the experienced parents, grandparents and relatives. A time of setting out and of radical change has begun in the young person.

Dear parents, you can compare your child with a young tree. The freshly planted tree still has to be tied to a stake so that it can become firmly rooted in the soil.

Something similar holds true for every child. During its first years on Earth, the small tree, your child, has been tied to the family trunk, figuratively speaking. Once the child has learned to walk and has gathered experiences, an inner force presses toward maturity, and then this small tree, the young person, wants to bear its own fruit. But until the fruit is ripe and falls from the tree – and another tree can develop from it – storms first come in the child's life. This means that the young person, the growing tree, frees itself slowly from the family trunk, in order to bear its own fruit. However, often, the first fruits are wild fruits. The tree is not yet refined, and the fruits are usually not yet edible.

Role model instead of authority

Dear parents, don't be disheartened and sad. The uncontrolled growth, the wild shoots, have to be pruned and the tree cultivated. But until this is possible, the turbulent young people have to try out their wild, inedible fruit, themselves. For many, this means "self-recognition through self-experience."

The life, into which the developing youth are growing, is their life. It carries all the traits of their soul, which come to light and call their attention to what they, themselves, have to change and clear up.

They experience their own positive and negative sides. The meaning of every life is: Recognize yourself and become divine again. The soul can mature only through self-recognition and actualization. The person refines their self, in order to bear good and beautiful fruit during later years of inner growth. The adult, as well as the youth, often still has to have bitter experiences, in order to reach self-recognition.

Dear parents, that is why I would like to advise you that during these stormy and stressful years not to be controlling, patronizing and authoritative with your child.

Remain calm despite the storms! Whatever your child was able to do during the first years of life on Earth that was noble and good is not lost. It remains in the soul and person and, unnoticed, has already taken root. The fruit will then ripen when the stormy and stressful time is over and the adult takes life into their own hands in order to master it.

Do not try to press your ideas on the youth and to pressure them into a certain pattern of thinking, because you think that you have to spare your child what you suffered in your lives.

Do not think that your child has to become what you, during your young years, wanted to become or what you missed during your young years. And do not think either that your child has to become such a hero, like grandfather was – or as quick-witted as your grandmother. Guard against seeing and wanting to have your child as you yourselves would have wanted to be seen.

Do not push your opinions onto your child. If you have the financial means for it, do not say, for example, that the young person could study this or that so as to attain a title or a name, for example, to become a doctor – or to learn another prestigious and lucrative profession. And do not think that the child has to realize the occupational desires that the father or the mother couldn't fulfill themselves.

With all these arguments and ideas that you want to talk the developing youth into, you will drive the young person out of your house. Instead, you should provide a real home for them, into which the young person can withdraw again and again, and in which they find security when they come into inner conflict.

Do not approach your developing youth with the usual educational methods of forbidding or commanding. The command will awaken in them if you yourselves are a good example.

Take the developing youth seriously. No longer see a child in them, but a developing and autonomous person who still needs some refinement.

Dear parents, you can best contribute to this refinement when you take your child seriously. Speak with them when the opportunity arises. Do not lecture them, because you think that your experience is also good for your child and could spare them a great deal. Certainly, it would be good if some of these experiences that the parents have made would be of use to the youth. But particularly during this period of storm and stress, in many cases, the youth have to go through their own experiences.

The parents' good example is the best advisor, better than good lessons, even if they are meant ever so well. Understated advice penetrates the youth's disposition more than admonishing, reprehensive and lecturing words.

Dear parents, be a good role model for your child, for they are gradually becoming an adult and also want to be seen and treated as such.

Strive to let the youth participate in decisive family conversations. Ask them what they think and endeavor to reach compromises when the young person's answer doesn't come as you expected.

In their arguments, you will certainly find useful and acceptable suggestions that you can respond to and consider.

Participation in these conversations strengthens the young people and gives them self-confidence. Knowing that they are accepted, that their thinking and ideas are acknowledged, gives them strength to think, to speak and to act ever more clearly in the future.

As a result of the conversations together and their participation in decisions, no matter of what kind, young people will also appreciate their parental home and will enjoy returning there.

The parents will then be good friends of the youth, with whom they can talk about many things, because they understand them and show understanding, and because the parents take them seriously and see them as a growing person, that is, as that which is ultimately urging them, namely, to be an adult.

Dear parents, if you accompany your child through life conscientiously, then it will not be difficult for you to be a good role model.

The child's conscientiously kept book of life is a self-revelation of their inner sensations, feelings and thoughts. Much can be recognized and deduced from the book of life. Through this, you are mostly familiar with your child's way of thinking. You know the wishes, the desires and the passions of your child. The content of the book of life lets you sense what is still hidden from the growing young person.

Besides this, the balance made after the child's ninth year of life, shows what has been accomplished and what has yet to be accomplished.

That is why, dear parents, it would be good if you would continue to keep your growing child's book of life. The prerequisite for this, however, is that your child, the growing young person, wants this.

If the child wants this, then from the ninth year onward, the book of life should be organized in a different way than until now.

Together with the growing child, it could now be kept as follows: The parents briefly report in the book of life what they recognize in the young person. Then, the youth also report what they learned each day, what they accomplished, that is, what they were able to clear up and what still needs to be taken care of.

And the times of exhilaration and depressions, the fits of anger and the nonsensical things in the growing youth's thoughts and desires, should also be kept in the book of life, including blazing enthusiasm.

All these are very decisive experiences of the young person, from which much can be deduced later on, especially with difficulties and even illnesses that could appear at a later time – but also the successes during their youth and adult life. A few notes every day about how and what the young person between nine and twelve is thinking, for example, which desires were expressed or why there was altercation and quarreling on this day – show their development.

With altercation and quarreling, it is very important to note down how the altercations and quarrels turned out, and what you, dear parents, could contribute to this.

Dear parents, don't note only the child's pros and cons in the book of life, the positive and negative things and expressions of your daughter or son – but also write how you, yourself, reacted to the fits of anger or to joyful, enthusiastic phases of the young person.

If you saw and assessed a matter falsely or if you were bad-tempered and angry over incidents and you acted unjustly toward the young person, then you should also make notes about this. Later on, when the child has grown up, especially these notes in the teenager's book of life about the parents' self-recognition awaken understanding and respect for the parents who have become their friends. Teenagers who have found friends in their parents find their way back to the parental home after the stormy and stressful period.

Thus, if the parents' weaknesses are also included in the daughter's or the son's book of life – namely, their wrong reactions to issues and behavior patterns of their child, then the young person or the adult will understand their parents and will remain connected with them. However, this will not happen if the parents write only their authoritarian thoughts in the book of life. In this way, they merely want to prove that they are infallible and the best parents in the world.

Those who want to put themselves in the right light will present themselves as they want to be seen. And every accusation that concerns one's neighbor indicates defensiveness. Those who believe that they are the best and infallible, and the other is the one who makes mistakes are ultimately the ones who lose. And those who defend themselves in this are accusing themselves.

When reading the book of life in the future, if such or similar thoughts and insights should be present, then the growing young person or the already adult son or daughter will find it difficult to see and accept their parents as good comrades and friends.

Every person has the urge to freely decide for themselves, because the soul of a person bears the law of freedom. The child's delicate and alert sensitivity accepts the parents' admission of a fault, whereas, however, it would rebel again and again against authoritarianism and feigned infallibility – and could thus develop a disturbed relationship with the parents and perhaps with fellow people. That is why, dear parents, show yourselves as you are and become good friends with your daughter or your son.

Daughter or son do indeed remain in your hearts as your child. But see yourselves in them.

Do you want to be treated as children? Certainly not. See in your children the same that you have in yourselves: the core of freedom, the urge for independence. It is the same desire of wanting to be taken seriously, which you have in yourselves. It is the same deep desire for peace and happiness.

Awaken peace and happiness in your growing children, by becoming their friend. Then your lives will run contentedly and happiness will stay with you.

Dear parents, endeavor again and again to talk with your child, with your son or daughter. Participate in your child's thinking and life. Then you will also recognize their joys and difficulties and can support and help them with selfless counsel in good time.

If your child's book of life was and is kept conscientiously, then it is possible to recognize, with the help of the notations, where the roots of possible difficulties are, that is, their cause. Often, what has been brought into this world from former lives is talked about, especially when difficulties arise. This should not be done too lightly in order to justify oneself. It should be recognized and, at the same time, the possibility for making amends: by clearing things up – by forgiving, by asking for forgiveness or by the application of positive thought powers.

To clear up a guilt possibly brought into this life, one has to first begin where difficulties arise: namely, in this earthly existence. Only when a person starts with the present situation does it become possible for them to find the causes from earlier lives.

If later on situations come up again that called up similar difficulties as during childhood, then these should be analyzed by the parents. It is possible that a situation not recognized by the parents or a wrong behavior elicits these difficulties again and again. Then a friendly talk with the son or with the daughter would be advisable in order to find the cause.

If the difficulties can be traced back to the fact that you, dear parents, were not in harmony in your life together, then you should tell your child this and apologize for it. The parents' realization can be the chance for the growing young people. They recognize their parents as friends who admit their mistakes and strive to make amends for what is still possible.

If the teenager or young adult experiences the parents as friends and not as infallible, authoritarian people who merely dominate and see the teenager, comparatively speaking, as a growing cell that may possibly produce rank and uncontrolled growth, which the parents have to attend to – then a warm communal life can develop.

Dear parents, please recognize that every young person first needs to be refined and to mature if they are to bear fruits as an adult.

Repetitions help us to remember. Therefore, I repeat: If the parents have become their children's friends and if these see a positive role model in the parents, then there will be frequent conversations, in which misunderstandings between parents and children can be cleared up and the positive aspects reinforced.

However, these conversations are inspiring, constructive and interesting for the young person only if in their own lives, the parents orient themselves positively and strive to uphold and actualize the law of selflessness. Out of this self-recognition and actualization of the divine laws, understanding and good will awaken toward one's own child, as well as toward all people. Understanding and good will are signs of inner authority and inner greatness. The inner greatness of a person results in love toward all people, humility and freedom. Out of this, can grow true friendships and togetherness, also with the families and relatives of already grown children. With their inner authority, generosity and tolerance, such people have a considerable influence on whole enterprises and large firms.

Generosity and tolerance grow out of alertness, clarity and nobility, but not out of indifference. They are the prerequisite for a lawful and purposeful leadership of people and companies.

People, who have mastered their lives and live according to God's laws are true messengers of a true humanity of which the Eternal speaks: "The old will pass away; I make all things new." The positive rises out of the negative.

People of the Spirit release the Spirit in matter. The Spirit rises out of the negative, out of humanness. This means that what is unlawful, what people created through their ego, will pass away. Instead of what is base and egocentric, the divine law will gradually be manifested through people who fulfill the Lord's will.

Humankind is in the midst of a time of radical change that has never existed before. Spiritual powers have an effect on matter and on humankind, and embrace all things, particularly people of good will.

The Spirit is released through God-filled people and brings about peace and harmony among the spiritually awakened. Positive powers will let the Kingdom of Peace become visible. These powers will see to it that ever more people fulfill the will of the Almighty.

Therefore, all parents are called – and it is placed upon you as a spiritual obligation – to bring up your children in such a way that they become useful people who master their lives without great problems and radiate positively and selflessly into their surroundings.

Dear parents, this doesn't mean that you should allow your children everything that they wish and want. A prudent guidance of young people is necessary. This guidance often has a positive and liberating effect only once they reach adulthood. Those who are honest with themselves and do not fool themselves are also open toward their fellow people. This is especially true in the family.

Free people who are not under the pressure of their own ego can speak openly about their weaknesses and mistakes, also to their children. Teenagers observe their parents and their surroundings in a very exacting way, for especially in puberty, many young people have a very fine perception of the genuineness of their fellow people's feelings, but also of false appearances, that is, of what is pretended.

Thus, dear parents, your growing children precisely sense when you merely pretend an ideal world to them, which, in fact, doesn't exist.

Hormones also influence the human senses of the growing teenagers, so that they now see the world as an adult perceives it, and no longer as the child saw and experienced it, which, until now, was well protected and cared for by the mother and father. Because of the hormonal effects on the senses, the growing teenager wants to get to know the world as, in many cases, adults see it: as a pasture for their passions and longings. The senses, pressing toward new horizons, still seek the secrets and mysteries of this world.

The fascination for the unknown and for what has not yet been experienced urges young people to go here and there. They want to experience the world as the majority of humankind experiences it.

When a young person has this urging, then they must experience the world as the masses see and experience it, and then draw their own conclusions from this. Through this, young people learn to make the right decision for their life. They get to know the world and themselves in the world. They have experiences and thereby experience disappointments. Both are important and instructive. In this way, they can gradually take their life into their own hands and set out on the path that is good for them at this time.

During quiet hours together, the son or daughter and the parents, as good friends, can frequently leaf through the book of life, in which many recognitions and actualizations are already recorded.

The young people growing up know that their parents, their friends, continue to keep the book of life and to make daily notes about their thoughts, life and their behavior patterns, so that if difficulties possibly arise later, the cause can be recognized and remedied right away.

The book of life also gives insights into childhood and shows how the young person, now growing up, thought and acted as a child. If the youth then decipher their earlier thinking, living and acting, they can perhaps then understand their present behavior. The book of life reflects the positive and the negative sides of the growing person and shows what the young person has already overcome.

The book of life is a book of self-recognition. Through it, it becomes clear how the divine laws and the law of cause and effect take place in the life of a person. As people think, that is how they are in their behavior and in their life; they surround themselves with what is the same or similar to themselves. This holds true not only for people, but, figuratively speaking, also for the souls in the worlds of the beyond.

A sentence which you can note: My thinking and actions lead me to people of like mind.

For the Young Brothers and Sisters

Personal experiences and decisions

Dear brother, dear sister, you will now gradually consider whether or not you will stay in the elementary school or should choose a secondary school.

Your sister Liobani has a question about this: Do you already have a wish for a certain occupation?

If so, then endeavor to have a look around every now and then in the occupation or the professional branch that you think would be right for you. Look around, see what life is like there, where you want to be someday to earn your living – and at a later time, perhaps not only for yourself, but also for your family. It is in the nature of things that a man takes a woman and that a woman is with a man.

Talk with your parents about your occupational wishes and then together, try to arrange things so that you can spend some hours during the week where you feel attracted to the occupation. If you have already engaged in artisan activities in school, if you have fun with writing or were even a small inventor, then you already have an inkling of individual professional fields. Recognize, however: Life in the world shows itself also from other sides. That is why it would be good if you could look around for a few hours at a time in other companies or facilities.

Dear parents, during this time of radical change from a child to a young person, from elementary school to a secondary school or a specialized school, it is important to maintain contact with the teachers. They have gotten to know your child from another side.

The growing youth should also be present now and then in these talks between parents and teachers, so that they don't become suspicious when father and mother talk about them with their teachers. The young person wants to be treated like an adult, that is, to be taken seriously.

Dear parents, your positive role model, which allows you to be above many things, gives you clarity and the right caring and constructive words in every situation, thus bringing about security in the young person.

If the children were guided and protected correctly, then they will come through this stormy and stressful time well. They know why they are on this Earth and will move forward consciously into their following years.

Young people in this time of storm and stress want to dance, for instance, and want to have acquaintances totally according to their ideas. They dream of the fulfillment of their desires, perhaps to become an ingenious person whom many look up to. The hope that their desires are fulfilled at fourteen, sixteen or eighteen years of age give them courage.

Dear parents, do not take the illusions from the young person, but strive to share with them the shadowed, as well as the light-filled, sides of human existence.

Speak very generally about mastering life and also about the advancements, defeats and disappointments of many great people. Even if the young people do not show any reaction to this, the senses and brain cells do store what they have heard and what they have already experienced themselves.

Every now and again, there is an opportunity to gain insight into the blows of fate and suffering of one's fellow people. This would also be good and advisable for a young person, so that they can picture this for themselves and shape their life's path in such a way that the same or similar things do not happen with them.

When you talk about blows of fate and thereby show how they are triggered, how they develop, build up and happen, the young person gains insight into the behavioral patterns of fellow people. At the same time, this stimulates and motivates them to think about their own way of thinking and living. If they happen to come into a similar situation later on, they will remember what they heard about other people who were also in such a situation. Via the senses and the brain cells, a young person then calls up what was formerly heard. This helps to set a new course in good time. The decision for their actions lies completely in them. If, however, the correct instructions for life were brought home to them during childhood – in a playful way and without coercion – then they will have developed a stable and positive decision-making ability and will be able to behave correctly according to the situation.

The soul brings with it the ability to decide lawfully and to act in a lawful way; however, this has to be awakened in childhood. According to its degree of maturity, the soul expresses itself through the person's disposition and senses. There, where it was before the incarnation, each soul in a human being was taught that it has to cleanse itself and find its way out of the law of sowing and reaping.

As long as people are under the influence of the law of sowing and reaping, they will be controlled by their soul's burdens. The soul is directed by way of the spiritual atoms, which, as a consequence of their burdening, have turned more and more toward the world, toward the external senses. The divine law, which is based on radiation, has an effect on the law of cause and effect. Through this, the burdens of the soul are touched and the person registers these in feelings, thoughts, words and actions. The burdens, the soul's guilt, also cause illnesses in the body as well as blows of fate.

By way of the brain cells and the senses, people are then directed by the causal law, the law of sowing and reaping. They look to where the causal law has them look. They listen to where their causes have them hear. They smell and stick their nose in where their causes compel them. Their sense of taste, the taste nerves, are also directed by the causes. They crave similar food and semi-luxury foods that they preferred in earlier lives or for which they had a longing and perhaps did not get, for whatever reason. They reach for and crave for things that they either owned in earlier lives or that they found pleasant or wanted to own back then.

People will continue to be directed by their burdens, which I also call correspondences, day after day, hour after hour and minute after minute, until they accept each day thankfully as their day and are open and thankful for the new recognitions that the day brings.

The energy of the day is the light of God. It wants to bring about a positive change of heart in every person, so that they recognize the true life, the true Being.

Those who accept their life daily and see every day as a gift of God, who strive to clear up everything that they have recognized, whatever is human, that is, not divine, will attain inner freedom and clarity of consciousness. Each day, each person is given precisely as much strength for self-recognition and actualization as they are capable of accepting and putting into practice.

The law of sowing and reaping works in an all-encompassing way. No person and also no soul can escape the fine mesh of the causal law. God's love radiates into this law of sowing and reaping; He does not want to overburden any of His children. The daily energy brings for each person as much as that person can deal with on that day. If, however, they do not heed the fine impulses that the day brings, if they do not heed their thoughts and emotions, then it is possible that the negative energies will consolidate into a complex and break in over them one day. These can be in the form of blows of fate, worries and sickness. They are then the sum of many impulses, warnings and aids that were not heeded. The person continued to sin. The burden can be the sum of many causes, in which the person did not heed the impulses, warnings and aids.

Thus, what was not cleared up can become an unbearable burden for a person because they wasted the days and did not ask why they are living. They did not work off what the day showed them in their thoughts and in the external occurrences, day after day.

Some will now ask: How should I know that the energy of the day has an effect on a part of my ego and admonishes me, so that I recognize myself and clear up what needs to be dealt with? May the following be said to this:

People have the divine laws. Many people go into the so-called churches, into stone houses, in order to give honor to God. Many read the Bible and the words of the

Sermon on the Mount. Many hear and read the mass media and can compare what is preached with what is lived. Many can hear and compare: How do the representatives of church and state speak and how do they act?

Everyone can ask themselves: How did Jesus of Nazareth live and what do the divine commandments say? Beyond that, at all times there were, and are, true prophets, the bearers of the word of the Spirit.

Someone who honestly endeavors to spiritualize their life, to recognize their fate, to master it in good time, before it has an effect on their body, will also be guided via their thoughts and senses, so that they find the way to that place for which they are thirsting. There is no excuse for the lethargy of the human ego and the carelessness of living each day as it comes and blaming your neighbor for your own worries, needs and illnesses. Your neighbor is not the guilty one, but everyone was and are themselves, the cause of all that happens to them. Those that are called the guilty ones often merely give the impetus, so that a cause may become visible or a request for forgiveness is stimulated. To what extent those who give the impulse – who were touched by the causal law and thus led, so that they gave the impulse to think about things – are karmically tied to the person concerned is contained in the law of sowing and reaping.

Be alert, dear brothers and sisters, and forgive the so-called "guilty one," so that you, too, may attain forgiveness, because basically, you are the guilty ones yourselves.

Dear parents, sooner or later, your child also has to recognize that not the other person is to blame, but always the one that has to endure the blow of fate and hardship. The earlier your child recognizes this, the easier it will be for the teenager, who looks toward the coming years with ideas, desires, expectations and smaller or greater castles in the air. Conversations about the law of sowing and reaping lay a good foundation for self-recognition and experiencing oneself. The young person between the ages of nine and twelve certainly has an interest in this. See to it that you do not express any threats, for example: If you do this or that, this or that will happen to you. The talks should be of a general nature, so that each one can get out of them what they think would be good for themselves.

Those who follow my suggestion to make it possible for a developing young person to see what it looks like in their dream occupation or occupations, can set the correct course for their future. As soon as a young person sees the occupational occurrences in the right light, many a decision becomes easier. They will then choose the occupation that corresponds to their capabilities and aptitudes.

Dear parents, the tasks and the responsibility for the child that is coming into puberty will not be less. Now you will see what you were able to give your children, with your sincere behavior, for their future years through life.

A saying on Earth goes: Small children, small worries, big children, big worries.

For those who brought up and directed their small child according to the rules of life of the eternal laws and was and is a good example, this saying is nothing more than a saying.

However, those who neglected their responsibility for, and care of, their child, and brought up the child without responsibility and without the guidelines of the Ten Commandments have made themselves guilty. In many cases, they have to experience that their child turns away from them because it experienced too little love.

A person who knows the laws of God and was a good mother or father to their child and a good teacher for the pupil, who was a role model through their own actualization, doesn't have to worry – not even when various human aspects break out of the soul, which touch the senses and influence the young person. The good, lawful foundation that was laid by the parents and teachers counteracts the awakening human ego.

When the hormones become more active and the child matures toward adulthood, various aspects are called up from the soul, from its burden. However, those who know that they and their child are in God's hand will care for their child in the right way.

This means: Do not be careless, but free of worry. Do not imagine all the bad things that could happen. If you see the future of your children only under the portent of your fear, then what you fear could actually happen. Surely you want to be a person free of worries.

The worldly person would have the following answers to my explanations: Then I am a successful person. But that is not quite so! Successful people, oriented to the world, are slaves to their intellect and believe only what they find to be good and right, that is, what they are able to understand. Such people are usually very narrow minded and, at the same time, intolerant. They accept nothing they cannot understand and that does not fit into their world of concepts.

These successes are limited. How long a purely human phase of success lasts depends on the light-filled and shadowed sides of the soul.

You should not become an intellectual person of success who is more authoritarian than an authority.

I wish for you that you become a spiritual authority who has inner leadership qualities and is capable and self-assured in their occupation, and whom their fellow workers also trust.

Spiritual authority means selflessness. It is spiritual self-assurance, which encompasses tolerance and understanding for one's neighbor.

Few are the people who are not authoritarian but are true authorities.

Most people are authoritarian; they dominate, tolerate no contradiction and constantly strive to exalt their human ego.

A true authority is a person with much empathy, with much understanding and tolerance toward their neighbor. They are a natural leader, dependable and by whom others let themselves be guided. They value and trust their colleagues at work.

Thus, recognize the difference between an authority and authoritarianism.

Authoritarian are such people who tolerate no contradiction, who are insubordinate and accuse their fellow people of being the guilty ones when something does not go as it should have. Authoritarian people quarrel a lot because they always want to be right when someone contradicts them.

Authoritarian people are limited; their consciousness is narrow, because they are oriented only to themselves. As long as their fellow people submit to their thinking and wanting, they maintain an external semblance of peace. However, if an egocentric, authoritarian person is contradicted, then the struggle for right and being right begins.

Authoritarian people constantly live in an area of conflict. They are usually discontent, because they are dependent on their neighbor's recognition. They are constantly concerned that their neighbors, their fellow people, confirm – that is, affirm – them in what they, the authoritarians, think is right.

Abilities, talents, qualities

Dear brother, dear sister, you have the best prerequisites for becoming a spiritually alert and open-minded person, with a good grasp of things, which includes selflessness and clarity.

You have used your childhood years and now you will also live through and experience your teenage years as they are and not as they seem to be for the people of this world.

You have either decided to stay in the secondary school or you have chosen to go on to a higher school. In both cases, the rule for the pupil is: "Your neighbor is also a person who is trying to make the best of their life." This means: Just like you, they also have faults and struggle to prove themselves in life.

The years between nine and twelve bring with them the first tests of character. You should get to know your fellow people properly and learn to value them. That's why it is important that you not become imitators who want to imitate or own what their neighbor may have, but which they do not have themselves.

Recognize yourself and explore your own abilities and qualities.

Do not look at your neighbor in order to copy from them what you do not have.

Find yourself: Find your abilities, your talents and qualities. Then you will become self-confident and in later life, a true authority. You will think clearly and logically and work in such a way that your fellow people will be satisfied with your work.

Dear brothers and sisters, the years go by. You have now become not only older, but also more mature. Your interests are now different than during childhood. Perhaps you also have new friends.

During the course of the years, people mature.

They take in impressions of their surroundings all according to their light-filled and shadowed sides. Many impressions are totally new for young people. They have to first accept them and come to terms with them.

Even if the impressions from childhood to the teenage years have changed and you now see your own small world in the mirror of your ideas and desires, despite all this, you should never forget that the soul in a person is on Earth to again become pure and selfless, an image of the heavenly Father, who created you and all pure beings.

At this time, you are a human being and should recognize your human condition. This shows itself in your ego, in the delimitation of mine and thine; it demands, wants to possess, to have and to be right. You should gradually give all this over to the Spirit of God in you. This also includes craving admiration, judging, condemning and disparaging others, in order to exalt yourself. If you can surrender this and overcome it, then the inner powers will become active in you and you will receive more life energy. Furthermore, the results include: clear and logical thinking, understanding and good will toward your fellow people. And in school, and later in your occupation, you will also be much more creative and spontaneous and will have a quick and precise grasp of things.

These are the positive traits of a spiritually alert and active person, who recognizes approaching situations in time and masters them.

Dear brother, dear sister, as you have heard, you should work for some hours in companies or administrations that you think could correspond to your choice of occupation, so that you get to know your abilities and qualities. Perhaps you have already visited companies and administrations and tested your abilities. If so, then write in your book of life whatever appealed to you, but also whatever did not. If you want your parents to also write in your book of life, then ask them to do so. Tell them of your experiences and recognitions.

What are the differences between abilities, talents and qualities?

Abilities can be manifold; then you have the skill to carry out this and that work in various occupational branches. Having the abilities for various areas of work does not mean, however, that you have the talent to make this your life's occupation.

We can compare the word ability with skill. Whoever has various abilities can help out here and there, when it is necessary.

Abilities alone do not fill out a future occupational life.

Many times, parents choose for their children, or the children choose themselves, an occupation according to their abilities. In many cases, adults as workers, employees, doctors, theologians, educators, company directors, technicians or engineers are not content, because the abilities that opened an occupational branch for them are often not sufficient to fill the whole job complex with joy.

In rare cases, talents are also artistic gifts. They can also influence the choice of an occupation. You have, for example, a talent for drawing and painting. You have a talent perhaps for handicrafts, without ever having been taught this or that; for instance, you take the right tool and create things that you never learned to make. Perhaps you even have the gift or talent to work with wood, to make pottery or the gift to create something beautiful out of a few remnants of cloth. All this and much more is a part of your talents.

If you see your abilities and talents together, then perhaps you can conclude which occupation would make you happy.

Qualities mean something beyond creating something of value out of the abilities and talents. So this means that if you have the quality to combine abilities and talents in such a way that a meaningful and valuable whole results from this, then you have combined abilities, talents and qualities in the right way.

A person often has many abilities and talents but is not able to combine these in the right way, so that something of value comes of this that you and your neighbor can use.

Due to their abilities and talents, people who have the predispositions for quality work see the whole task in front of them, even before they begin the work. You have, for instance, the special ability and talent to draw or to carve a flower, a bush or an animal. If you also have a predisposition for quality, then an artistic work will be produced, which will be valued by your neighbor and your environment. The talents, abilities and qualities should be seen as a whole and always taken into consideration, so that all the prerequisites for an occupation can be accounted for. Only when people choose their occupation in accordance with all three aspects will they be fulfilled and satisfied in their occupation.

The child's book of life can again help to explore the talents, abilities and qualities.

I add the following reference points, in order to recognize and discern them in the child's book of life.

The small child's behavior patterns with a favorite toy or doll indicate talents, qualities and abilities. They also show in which situations and in which way the child was kind, strict or even rejecting toward its favorite. What did the child whisper to it in the child's exuberance or during sad hours?

Which qualities, talents and abilities did the child develop in smaller and larger duties, in the house or outside in the garden, while shopping or at school?

How did and does the child behave with teachers and schoolmates?

How did and does the child behave with passersby in the street and in the means of transportation?

Which characteristics of parents, teachers and classmates did, and does, the child accept as a given? Which does the child affirm and which are categorically refuted?

Against what or against whom does the child rebel?

How and what does the child say about its fellow people?

Which character does the child value in people and which are rejected or repudiated with fits of anger or hate?

Dear parents, write all this down in the book of life and analyze the whole complex. Especially the years between nine and twelve say a great deal!

Those who have taken, and take, the thinking, speaking and acting of their child seriously, who carry the responsibility for the life of their child have made the effort to keep the book of life conscientiously, and will also now be able to work out the abilities, talents and qualities from it.

Dear parents, if you have done this, then compare them with the curriculum of the chosen school and the present occupational and training wishes of the teenager. By this, it may be possible to find out whether the young person has chosen the right school.

The book of life can also be shown to the responsible teacher when it is time to talk with them about the wishes for, or choice of, an occupation. The child's behavior in the various school subjects is also informative in terms of the correct choice of an occupation. That is why the teacher should also be included in the choice of occupation.

Finding yourself

Dear brothers and sisters, you are now teenagers. A question to you:

Which characteristics indicate a spiritually awakened and level-headed young person?

How do growing young people encounter adults and older people?

They respect their fellow people. They do not laugh at them or make fun of them when they say or do something that is not pleasing or that seem to be ridiculous or inappropriate.

Dear brother, dear sister, never laugh about the idiosyncrasies of older people. Who knows how you will be!

You are now gradually beginning to determine your own life. You are outgrowing your parent's care and want to take your own life in hand and live as you believe to be correct. Check your thinking and your actions, also during this stormy and stressful time, as well as your behavior toward other people.

Recognize that at this point you are still in a phase of upheaval from being a child to becoming a youth and after that, from being a young person to becoming an adult. Today you think in one way and tomorrow you will already think differently. This is especially pronounced as long as you are dependent on the opinions, ideas and desires of other people. Not every older and mature person who, in your eyes, seems odd sometimes, had the opportunity in their youth to be taught according to the spiritual laws, as you were instructed and guided. In many situations of life, many of these older and seemingly odd people relied on the opinion of others, were disappointed, and again leaned on other people. In this way, they failed to develop their spiritual aspects and qualities. Anxious, frightened and disappointed in life, many have let their lives go by. Speak with people whom you think are odd. Then, among other things, you will recognize what you can do better in your life on Earth.

Perhaps in your circle of relatives, there are aunts and uncles whom you reject, because you think that their way of looking at life is eccentric, and in many cases, you cannot accept their obstinacy in claiming something when it comes to their own personal lives. Perhaps you think it would be a waste of time to have anything to do with them. Oh no! Learn to empathize with such people, and then you will recognize that in some cases, they did not have the right guidance during childhood, that perhaps they were brought up in an authoritarian way and were therefore intimidated – or that they regret their past or are angry about it.

Many older people recognize that their lives should have gone differently and are sad about it. They have to recognize that life's clock cannot be turned back. They think that their life has passed them by, or that they were cheated out of their lives, because, as they say, others, perhaps their parents, had a determining influence upon them.

Let's look at it from the point of view of the ethical, moral principle and of the eternal law: Many people are not aware of their responsibility for their life and for that of their neighbor. They simply take each day as it comes and see their faults, which the day wanted to show them, only in their fellow people.

During their youth, many an older person also thought as you do – and now, have become just as they thought about their neighbor back then. Although there frequently are people who have a deeper insight into the meaning of life and into the law of cause and effect and talk about it – and although there are many books about it – few people want to deal with this. And when they hear about it, they want to keep their customary way of thinking and living, because it is more comfortable.

It is also more comfortable to blame others for your own fate and wrongdoing, than to look for this in yourself and begin with yourself. But in this way, people do not find the way to their real life. As long as they blame their neighbor for this, they often believe that others had cheated them out of their life; for example, because the parents were authoritarian, they were not able to fulfill their wishes.

That is possible, but all people, and be it only once reaching adulthood, are always given the possibility to turn around in time and to improve their life's qualities.

However, those that constantly look to their neighbor and imitate what they would like to be or have will never find themselves, and will pass by their own life, remaining an imitator.

Such people do only what other people think is correct. They bind themselves to the opinions and ideas of others and do not discover their own abilities, talents and qualities.

Such people pass their life by; they are lived by others, by those who want to let their opinions and ideas take form in these imitators. These are the authoritarians who make slaves of those servile to them. The dependents let themselves be enslaved because they are too lazy to work on themselves.

Such people know neither their true nature nor themselves as a person with their own thoughts and desires. There are enough such slaves who are lived by others, because they look only to their neighbors and imitate them – and ultimately are dominated by them.

These are the people who are dissatisfied with their lives, who are already old and odd when middle-aged, because they were disappointed in life – so they believe. In this way, they remain stuck to their past and no longer see what the present holds ready for them in the way of friendliness, good will, freedom and peace.

Dear brother, dear sister, especially in younger years, from the age of nine onward, when the hormonal activity increases, the light-filled and shadowed sides of your soul also become more active and have an effect on you.

The increased activity of hormones also stimulates your sensory organs, your senses of sight, hearing, smell, taste and touch. What you did not notice before, you begin to register with your senses. This stronger sensory perception has an effect on the burdens of the soul as well as on the pure areas of the soul, both of which thus become more active. Via the person's brain, they irradiate, in turn, the senses, the feelings and also the desires that were hidden until now. It is through this that the person receives the possibility to correctly recognize the positive and the negative predispositions and inclinations from the soul that are becoming active – in order to overcome the negative, and to lawfully apply and utilize the positive. If they themselves have gained experience and wisdom in life, then experienced parents and educators can be a valuable support for the young person.

Dear brother, dear sister, that is why it is good if you regard your parents and understanding teachers as your friends who support you, who advise you and convey to you in conversation what is worth thinking about. So as not to become an imitator, whose life is lived by others, maintain the good friendship of selfless, experienced people, who help you to ascertain your abilities, talents and qualities.

Treasure good friends and preserve good friendships, which should mean: Speak with your fellow people about their experiences and include your knowledge and your actualization. Do not be determining and intolerant if the conversation takes another course than you would have liked or when it is no longer interesting to you. Practice conversing and endeavor to make it interesting or to keep it on an appropriate level. This is possible for you if you pose skillful questions, which frequently stimulate new aspects.

Also practice this. Then you will experience yourself and realize that every person is on a different level in life and that they are also struggling with themselves, and that no one who is oriented to the world is great.

I, Liobani, wish for you that you become great in spirit and filled with divine wisdom and love; for there are still few such people.

I said, "There are still few." In the time of spiritual awakening, in which many people strive for higher ideals and values, there will be ever more great people, who draw from God's All-power, who teach the eternal, cosmic law in this world and also personify this in word and deed. If you also want to be one of these, then be mindful of your thinking, speaking and acting.

Recognize yourself and become selfless!

Set yourself the goal not to become an imitator, but to shape your life in such a way as it has been given to you by your origin, by the Spirit of God.

Find the positive in all people and address it in you and in your fellow people.

Build no castles in the air, but analyze your thoughts and desires. This means, take a good look at them to see if they can be realized, that is, carried out. You will certainly be able to talk about this with good friends.

I repeat: Parents, relatives and educators should be good friends to a young person, people who merely exercise an advisory function and do not want to lecture or even dominate.

Setting a course

ear brother, dear sister, you are now setting a course for your life as an adult.

Surely you have planned a great deal for your life on Earth. At your age, the growing youth are of the opinion that they can do many things better in life than the adults, of whom they know are dissatisfied with their lives and consequently, often begin and end their day in a grumpy and cantankerous way.

Dear brothers and sisters, every person and every soul, every one of them, has to realize one day that they do not live in the temporal so as to enjoy life to the fullest, that is, to get rid of all manners and morals and to be unrestrained and self-indulgent.

A person should realize why their soul is in an earthly garment, that is, a human being.

If people accept the day as it is given to them and make the best of it, then they will remain youthful and dynamic from within, well into old age.

Your soul is in a physical body. You are a human being in order to again learn the high ideals and values of the soul, of the Kingdom of God, and to be able to live in freedom, health, happiness and contentment. Who does not wish this?

All people long for happiness, security, contentment, health, money and possessions. Most people put all their respective forces into fulfilling their earthly wishes. Most of them have to work hard; others build up positions of power for themselves or profit from their inventions or do not shy away from intrigues and fraud.

To fulfill such worldly desires is often merely an illusionary gain. Many a one who works hard and saves can indeed afford more in this world than others; if, however, you gain insight into their way of thinking and living, you see that despite their worldly goods, they are dissatisfied and often even unhappy. True contentment comes from within and from a lawful and straightforward life.

Many people are of the opinion that whoever has money, wealth and prestige owns the world. That is why they strive for power and positions of power, so that they may influence their fellow people and move them here and there as they see fit, like toy figures. Others, in turn, have a lot of money and believe that they are better than those who have less. However, those who are of the opinion that money and possessions are everything are poor in spirit, even if their fellow people respect them because of their money and prestige. However, prestige is attained by them only from those who speculate on their money or who expect help from them for their own ends.

With all the striving for material ends, spiritual qualities and the spiritual ideals and values waste away more and more. Such people are poor in their inner being, because they strive only for external things and therefore, are never satisfied. They are dissatisfied, and constantly on the lookout to gain more and to keep more. Rich people have very few selfless friends. Their friends are usually those who own just as much, or such, as are good friends of their money.

True, selfless friendship is what you, dear brothers and sisters, should strive for. True friends form an inner community, in which one can depend on the other. Therefore, strive to learn an occupation that brings you joy and not one with which you want to acquire external things.

Find true friends. You will find them if you are honest with yourself and with your neighbor, if you don't expect anything from them, but actively participate in the relationship.

Never strive for prestige and lots of money merely to gain material things, as I have just described. Otherwise, you will remain or become poor and lonely in your inner being; for those who are seemingly your friends want to bask in your prestige and profit from your money. You recognize very well that these are not true friends. They can be compared to vines that wind themselves around bushes and trees and, in time, suck them dry more and more, until they can hardly live any longer, therefore producing ever fewer blossoms and fruit. In many examples and comparisons, nature shows human beings how they should think and live: Egocentric and power-hungry people are very similar to vines. They ensnare the people that are servile to them by flattering them; however, they do this for their own sake, in order to achieve what they want to hear personally or to possess, for example, money, possessions and prestige.

Dear brother, dear sister, life's fruits, the inner ideals and values, should radiate out of you and should be externally visible in your selflessness. That is true humanity and heroism.

That is why you should learn an occupation that brings you joy and corresponds to your abilities, talents and qualities.

If it is your desire to serve your neighbor with your occupation and not to merely gain money and possessions, then you are on the right path.

True and noble fruits are those that come from a person's inner being. Such people do not work solely to accumulate money and possessions for themselves, but in order to build a healthy community and economic life.

If you have acquired or inherited a lot of money, then don't keep everything for yourself. In the long run, it will bring you little happiness and little inner contentment. Use a large part of it for the general good and live like the general public, not in poverty, but as part of a good middle class.

If you set up your life on Earth in this way, you will also find true friends who accept you as their neighbor and not only because of your money.

Money and possessions do not belong to the human being. God gives them to people so that they put a greater part of it to use for the general good, thus helping poorer people, and not so that they can play the master and regard others who have less as servants.

The rich who hold on to their wealth and thus bind themselves to it, whose only striving is to increase it for their personal purpose will not enter the Kingdom of God. According to the law of sowing and reaping, their souls will continue to come into this world, that is, they will incarnate, until they have learned selflessness and no longer put themselves above their fellow people, but apply the principle of equality and brotherliness.

The principle of equality is a heavenly law. No divine being has more or less than the others. Each one has all of infinity as essence in itself. This is the richness of the inner being, which expresses itself in the external world.

In the Lord's Prayer, Christians pray: "on Earth as it is in heaven." With the words, "Your kingdom come, Your will be done," they ask for equality. The law of the heavens is the balance of powers, which brings about equality.

If some people have considerably more assets than others and call these assets their own, then, before the great, almighty law of equality, they are truly poor devils. Sooner or later, they will be poor, for what they bind to themselves, what they call their own, they will lose. They have perhaps inherited a lot of money and possessions in this life; in the next life they will be the poor devils, who then may learn to earn the energies through the law of "pray and work." With energies, I mean the money of human beings.

Thus, in the next life, a rich person today may then learn what it means to work honestly and to become selfless. Therefore, do not set your personal goals and your desires too high and do not let them wander too far out into this world.

Keep your feet on the ground of reality and strive to become a good and useful adult, people with inner ideals and values who affirm their fellow people as a part of themselves.

Selflessness

Dear brother, dear sister, so that you recognize life as it is you can now gather many experiences. You can practice selflessness and experience how it affects you and your immediate surroundings.

Begin to experience the law of God, the selfless love, on yourself. Practice this by doing small selfless deeds.

You have heard: Each day is your day. It brings you feelings, thoughts and wishes. That is your daily energy, which you once sent out. Good things and less-good things come with your day, all that you projected into the atmosphere in this life or in an earlier one. They are your feelings, thoughts, words and deeds. Thankfully accept the impulses that your day brings. Put the good impulses into practice and clear up the human impulses, either by asking for forgiveness for what you committed or by forgiving the pain that was caused to you.

Begin to practice selflessness. On your way to school or in school, you have the possibility again and again to do good without expecting thanks or reward. For example, you can help an older person cross the street or be helpful when they get out of a streetcar. You can also help your teacher when there is much work that you can do. You can also run small errands and services for a small sum and give a part of this to poor and needy people; or you can selflessly give joy to someone you know. You can also make a small donation to an organization that helps animals, or in winter, hang up bird feeders in the garden as well as in the woods, thus ensuring that the birds have food, which you buy partly from your allowance. You can do all this and much more to practice selflessness.

If you have acted selflessly without expecting thanks and reward, then check yourself to see what you felt and feel thereby.

You can also get together with a friend and run errands for older people. If you do this together conscientiously and selflessly, then at the end of the day you will realize how happy, cheerful and content you are. You feel better than if you had worked for thanks and reward, because you have become richer in your inner being. However, that should not mean that you merely do odd jobs and do not learn an occupation. Oh no, it is good to have an occupation that brings joy.

This advice, to experience selflessness, will also help you in school and later in your occupation. From the experiences with people, from the small earnings and selfless help, you get to know people and their fortune. With these small and greater selfless services, you will gain understanding for many people and also learn to love the animals. When you are then grown up, many an experience from your youth will help you get over the obstacles in life.

Your egocentric thinking, which relates only to your well-being, will recede more and more. People who have practiced and practice selfless love think above and beyond the small horizon of their human ego, because in their selfless efforts, they understand many of their fellow people and because, at your age, they have already gathered experiences. Out of the experiences and occurrences with your neighbor, you also learn how you should be and think, what is egocentric and what is selfless.

Dear brother, dear sister, with this advice I do not want to keep you from the carefree life of youth. Oh no, quite the contrary: Be that young person who looks into the world with alert senses and learns to differentiate reality from illusion.

You should be happy and cheerful; you should leap and hop, play games and go hiking and show yourselves as you are, quite naturally – just as young animals are. Young people are sometimes like young, unbridled foals who are still carefree, yet galloping into the world, filled with expectations.

Therefore, do experience the world. However, observe it objectively – as a person who has already gathered experiences with selflessness and their first small earnings.

This should also be repeated: Please do not become an imitator! If you keep what I have just advised you: If you practice selflessness, do small tasks, have already earned a small amount and take over short-term activities, in order to get to know your abilities, talents and qualities, this will give you experience and insight. You will thereby discover yourself more and more; you will expand your abilities, talents and qualities and will not be an imitator, who wants only what other people want or possess. You will not build any castles in the air, but will see the world – which now shows itself to you, the youth, from another side – as it is. You will learn to better classify and understand new impressions. You will also develop a friendly relationship with older people who are no longer odd to you, due to your smaller and greater experiences with them. Nor are they so far away from your own thinking. With the small, selfless errands, you have gotten to know, to understand and also to appreciate older people.

If you are alert from within, you are not so preoccupied with yourself and with your wishes, and you experience each day differently. For each day is rich in experiences and recognitions.

It would be good and would contribute to a friendship between your parents and you, if you talk with them about your daily experiences and write the most important things in your book of life or ask your parents to do this for you.

Between the ages of nine and twelve, the day will now go somewhat differently. This begins already when you awaken in the morning. Your mother no longer has to take care of every little thing.

Because you are now becoming more and more independent, I may also advise you to get up a quarter of an hour earlier, and after you have washed and dressed, before breakfast, to withdraw into your room and pray to God, our Father.

Place the new day and everything that it will bring you in His loving hands.

And place into God's hands your parents and teachers, and all the people that you will meet and with whom you will have something to do on this day.

Ask God that He support and help you in school and turn to your guardian angel as well, if you are faced with difficult tasks or even exams.

You should talk with your guardian angel often; they are good, faithful, invisible friends at your side. They are with you; they protect you and want to help you in every situation. They help you out of smaller and greater difficulties. They are also at your side when you do homework and take exams. But do think of them, also when you are joyful and have success.

Your guardian angel is with you and has not only been sent by God, our heavenly Father, to stand at your side, to help you and serve you, but also to admonish you if you view something incorrectly or do something wrong.

Therefore, pay attention to your spiritual, invisible friend.

First of all, however, honor and thanks are due to God, our Father. So early in the morning, before breakfast, give thanks to God for everything that the new day brings. Surrender to God, our Lord, all that lies before you and of which you already know will come to you today, and afterward talk about this with your guardian angel, your spiritual, light-filled friend. Ask your guardian angel to support you in the name of the Lord. Strengthened through God and guided by God and your guardian angel, you then begin the new day.

When things come to you during the day that you don't really know how to grasp, to recognize and how to tackle, pray to God and speak to your invisible friend, your guardian angel. Your guardian angel helps you according to the laws of God, of our heavenly Father.

Who is Liobani? – The spirit beings

erhaps you have already asked if I, Liobani, am also a guardian angel.

I am not a guardian angel who accompanies people and protects them. Instead, I am a teaching angel in the four spiritual development planes of the heavens. Here, many light-rays meet, unite, and in further development become spiritual minerals. In the heavenly worlds, the plants gradually develop from the spiritual minerals. And then, from these plants, the spiritual animal world, and from the animal forms, then in a long evolutionary process, the elemental beings of heaven.

I would like to describe briefly to you what all I, Liobani, have to do in the development planes, so that you may recognize that all of infinity is oriented toward selfless service.

As a matured nature being, I was born into the divine ray of Wisdom. That means that I came out of the ray of Wisdom as a spirit child. Thus, I am a child, a daughter of the divine Wisdom.

Like all other spirit children, as a spirit child, I once more activated in me all the heavenly planes, that is, vivified them, and at the same time, developed the three filiation attributes more strongly. In this world, the three filiation attributes are called Patience, Love and Mercy.

During this evolutionary process from the spirit child to the matured spirit being, I recognized that my spiritual mentality – you would say my attributes, abilities, talents and qualities – is in the care of spirit children, namely, in the evolutionary sphere of the four spiritual development planes.

When on their evolutionary path, the spirit children activate the seven basic rays of God and go through the four development planes once again in order to also vivify these powers more strongly, then I am – as well as many other teaching beings – responsible for them:

We endeavor to have them once again live through their former life of development, the becoming and growing from the mineral up to the spiritual birth, to a spirit child. Through this spiritual training, the connection to all forms of Being is reinforced in the spirit child.

Thus, how do the spirit children learn?

Children in the eternal Being, in the Kingdom of God, learn the way the children in this world should also learn, not in theory, but in practice.

The spirit children do not sit at desks in school, in order to theoretically learn the subject matter or to write down things very neatly or even to learn things by memory.

You have heard that in all of infinity everything is consciousness. Spiritual minerals, plants, animals, stars and spirit beings are consciousness.

When the spiritual children – with a spiritual child, I mean a spiritually self-activating, luminous, radiating body – activate in themselves the consciousness of the minerals, plants, animals and nature beings, that is, when they vivify them more strongly, then they are in this consciousness field in order to connect with these consciousness spheres. They let the forces of the spiritual essences of minerals, plants, animals and nature beings flow into their spirit body and receive further energy for their body in this way. This brings about the maturing process and the growth of the spirit child. Therefore, the spirit children are where the divine energies are forming, that is, where they are assuming spiritual forms.

As you have already heard, your spiritual body, that is, your soul, is developed through a spiritual atom, a light-ray. The structure of the spiritual body emerges via the spiritual minerals, plants, animals and elemental spirits, which are also called elemental beings. A spirit child has already developed all this in itself.

However, the spirit child now perceives its spirit structure even more consciously. It recognizes itself as a child of God-Father, who is its primordial Father and primordial Mother.

The matured nature being was taken into the bosom of the parents by a dual pair, a spiritual parental pair, and became their spiritual child, which they dedicated to the primordial Father, the Father-Mother-God.

The child now develops into the matured spirit being, by once again vivifying in itself the primordial sensations of the spiritual minerals, plants and animals. As a spirit child, it likewise intensely absorbs the connection to the elemental beings again, of which it once was itself. Thus, it again experiences in itself the evolution of minerals and plants, and how during the course of further and greater actions of light, ever more perfect forms are developed out of the still shapeless plant, animal and elemental forms. As a spirit child it experiences once more the rhythm of evolution.

This absorption of the evolutionary process is done in that the spirit child helps the evolution by serving the small, still shapeless spiritual forms; for example, by supporting a plant species during the changeover from the plant form to the initial animal form.

You could also see the spiritual evolution from the plant to the developing animal as a rebirth, which is similar to a birth. The spirit children help directly with this wonderful evolutionary event. The result is unity, the absolute, lawful "state of being interwoven and intertwined" of the spirit being with all forms of life.

The spiritual children of the Kingdom of God go through all heavenly planes, thereby, once again establishing the spiritual connection to all that they bear within as spirit children. This means that they now intensify what they have absorbed during their evolutionary path from a mineral to a spirit child. In the heavenly planes, they also intensify their understanding of the workings of the divine laws and the procedure of the heavenly mechanics. In this way, they get to know all the details of the function of the Absolute Law. At the same time, their spirit bodies become ever more active. Thereby, their mentality, that is, their particular spiritual abilities, are awakened.

The universal law also encompasses the whole heavenly system of communication. This means that every spirit being is in constant communication with all cosmic energies and can see in itself all that is taking place in all of infinity. It does not have to be in the same place to see these cosmic processes or to make contact with another spirit being. It sees everything in itself. There is no "place" in all of infinity, because everything is in everything else, also in each spirit being. Therefore, the spirit being experiences all of infinity in itself. It is aware of every ray and every spiritual principle. This intense absorption of the whole cosmic radiation makes the spirit child itself the law of God, and therefore, divine.

For this spiritual training of the spirit child, which immediately experiences, sees and applies in itself everything that it recognizes, it needs neither a "school desk" nor theoretical lessons. It learns, experiences, lives and beholds all in one.

This spiritual maturing of the spirit child is its growth. To the same extent that the spirit child absorbs the radiation, the heavenly mechanics, all seven basic powers of the universe, including the four spiritual development planes, so does its consciousness expand. In infinity everything is absolute consciousness. The spirit child gradually develops its full consciousness, thus becoming a matured spirit being.

As soon as a matured nature being has been raised to the filiation of God, that is, has been received by a spiritual dual pair, you would say by a spiritual parental pair, and has attained the filiation through this parental pair, it is a spirit child and no longer a nature being. It is no longer on the reserve to which it was connected as a nature being.

During this training, the spirit child awakens all seven basic heavens in itself, to which the three attributes of filiation, Patience, Love and Mercy, belong. Once the spirit child has opened up the seven basic heavens with the four development planes, it is a bearer of the absolute consciousness, from which the absolute free will results. Thus, its will is no longer latent, as in the developing forms of minerals, plants, animals and elemental spirits.

With the development of the absolute freedom of will, the spirit child has become a matured spirit being that lives the eternal law in all details. It has then become the law of God, itself.

Dear human child, see, your soul has already gone through all these details that I have explained to you. In you, in your human person, a matured spirit being exists that knows the total heavenly mechanics and that is connected to all Being. With the incarnation of your spirit body into the material body, in accordance with the eternal law, much of your origin was covered up.

Furthermore: During your development as a human being, you have burdened yourself. During the alternation of incarnations, you transgressed against the law, God, and in this way, the burden covered up the heavenly law in you, again and again. That is why the knowledge about the system of communication with the divine powers has been lost to you as a human being. However, all of infinity lies hidden deep in your soul. And now, as a human being, you have the task and many possibilities to recognize the shadows in your soul and to overcome them through the Spirit of Christ, the redeeming power, so that the eternal laws break through in you once more.

You can talk with your parents or with good friends about why you became a human being and why you burdened your soul. From the many revelations of the eternal Lord and His servant, the heavenly prince and law-angel of the divine Wisdom, called Brother Emanuel on Earth, your parents and friends know about the Fall-event, the Fall of the Angels. This was triggered by one angel that wanted to be like God and had to leave the pure heavens. With it went many spirit beings that let themselves be convinced by it. Besides this, since the Fall of the Angels, over the course of time, many spirit beings have come from the heavens into incarnation – that is, they incarnated into an earthly garment – in order to help and serve the disobedient and unfaithful Fall-beings. With this, however, as human beings, many helpful spirit beings succumbed to the temptations of the darkness, which, via the senses, the feelings, thoughts, words and deeds, crept and creep into human beings. They misled, and mislead them, so that it was, and is, no longer possible for them to recognize and follow God's laws.

The unlawful feeling, thinking, speaking and acting then resulted in a burden. That is why many incarnated spirit beings that came to Earth to help make a breakthrough, like the Fall-beings, now have to go the Inner Path to the Kingdom of God under similarly difficult conditions.

This was a short overview of the Fall-event, so that you may have some points to start with for such a conversation.

Certainly, your parents or friends have read various things about this and perhaps even experienced themselves, how the "Satan of the senses," the darkness, which shuns the light, wants to lead people astray and does lead them astray.

It stands to reason that as a pure being you once wantedto help the fallen spirit beings in an earthly garment – but as a human being you burdened yourself, because you surrendered your senses, feelings, thoughts, words and actions to the world without control, and the Satan of the senses was able to lead you astray. This can happen, for example, in that you sought after money and possessions and thereby, perhaps cheated your neighbor so that your plan worked. Or you disparaged your fellow people by talking badly about them. You did this to exalt your own person. Or you stole from or even murdered your neighbor. Know that whoever deliberately kills animals also murders.

See, the many ugly, hateful thoughts and the many loveless acts cover over the beauty, the selflessness and the goodness of the soul.

Everything that is against selfless love, for example, hatred, quarreling, strife and animosity are satanic features. They cause separation among the people; from this, weapons are produced and wars break out.

Recognize that individuals cannot fight against the satanic, the darkness, by merely talking about it. They themselves have to deal with it and declare war on their own base feelings, thoughts, words and desires and defeat them with the power of Christ.

Only when it has become brighter in the souls and people, are they a guiding light and a selfless example for their neighbor. Only in this way, will it become more light-filled and brighter in this world, on this Earth, and the people will find their way to one another in love.

It will not become more light-filled in this world by talking and not through prayer alone, but through a lawful life, in which the people actualize the divine that they talk about – and by fulfilling what they prayed for, themselves. Therefore, begin with yourself first.

I, Liobani, have given you advice. Now it depends on how much you accept and actualize.

You must know that the soul of every person returns to heaven, to the homeland, only once it has become flawless. You determine yourself when this will be.

That every physical body will reach death is certain. It is the passing away of the body. However, your soul bears within itself what you have caused or cleared up, the light-filled sides and the shadowed sides of your life on Earth. Whatever you have not cleared up as a human being is taken by the soul into the beyond. That is its baggage. It comes back into this existence, into a physical body, with this burden, if it was not able to pay off some of it in the soul realms. For this reason, make use of the time, the hours and the minutes.

Thus, you have learned that God, our heavenly Father, endeavors through your Redeemer, Christ, that you as a human being clear up your burdens on Earth and program your brain cells neither with just a lot of knowledge, nor with a lot of desires and longings, but rather, that you practice putting into practice, that is, actualizing, what you have recognized. In this way, you learn to know the life in this world and also learn to discover your abilities, talents and qualities early enough, and will then choose an occupation that fulfills and completes you. And you will build no castles in the air!

Christ, the Redeemer of humankind, builds the Kingdom of God on Earth through His faithful ones, through people who first seek the Kingdom of God in themselves – and find it by actualizing the holy laws, by thinking and doing what is noble and good. This inner kingdom will come through people who strive to fulfill God's will. On Earth, it will also encompass what is necessary for the production, for instance, of shelter, clothing, food and much more. That is why, in God's Kingdom on Earth, there will be artisan enterprises of various trades. The person learns to put the divine laws into practice by fulfilling the law, "Pray and Work." The artisan enterprises will be based on the principle of divine harmony. Here, a person learns to think, to live and to work correctly. It will be much easier for those who have experienced a spiritual development since childhood.

That is why I advise. Do you accept?

Those who actualize the divine laws more and more belong in the true brotherhood of Christ.

People in the brotherhood of Christ live together and are for one another – and not against one another.

Families that are devoted to one another in love live in it. As the positive giving power, the man will honestly nourish and protect his family. In the harmony of two poles, the male and female principles, the woman will be the guardian and keeper of what the man, the positive giving power, has created with her. Both man and woman, will complement one another and be devoted to one another in selfless love, in understanding and faithfulness. That is why they will also be good parents, comrades and friends to their children.

The mountain spirit

As a growing youth, you will wander through woods and fields. Or you will experience mountain hikes with your parents, a teacher and your school friends. Please don't forget that nature lives. Every flower, every animal feels, even the most inconspicuous stone senses your radiation. Life feels, in turn, life – that is the communication of positive powers.

Now I will tell you a few things about the mountain spirit, so that you will also gain knowledge about this elemental power and when you spend your holidays in the mountains, or go on a tour of them, you will know that in God, everything has its order.

The mountains are also divided into reserves because the nature beings also perform their services in and on the mountains. The mountain spirit is at work high up in the rocky areas where there is hardly any vegetation.

The mountain spirit is the inner life of the mountains. The consciousness of the mountain spirit consists of the spiritual essence of stones and minerals. Every kind of stone and every mineral is consciousness. Everything that took on and takes on form from the eternal streaming Spirit is a spiritual manifestation and the consciousness state of this form. Consequently, the various spiritual substances that are present in the stones and minerals have consciousness. The totality, for example, the stone, as such, is called consciousness. The mountain spirit is the consciousness of the innumerable stones and minerals of a mountain.

A greater or lesser mountain massif is a reserve. The nature beings are also active here. The mountain spirit can take on the corresponding form of the stone and mineral consciousness, just like the elemental spirits of fire, water and air. The fire spirits as well as the water and air spirits, and likewise the mountain spirit, can then, according to their consciousness, take on form or pass into the streaming All-power as consciousness potential. On the other hand, plants, bushes, trees and animals remain tied to their form. Nature beings also remain manifested ener-

gy, because the so-called elves and dwarfs are already on the preliminary step to the filiation of God.

The elemental spirits of fire, water, earth and air, which only give a hint of a form, can let their first unformed and merely implied forms flow back into streaming energy, as can the mountain spirit. However, they show themselves now and again in their spiritual evolutionary forms, especially when they are called by the nature beings, the elves and the dwarfs, and asked for help. They give themselves a form according to their consciousness, also when the elemental spirits come together to pray, for instance, for the sun dance, in order to worship the All-Spirit.

The mountain spirit can also give itself a form. It appears as a mighty figure, which is much bigger than the giant that you know from your fairy tales. When it takes on a shape and strides over the mountains, then it is usually very high up where there are only cliffs, rocks and little vegetation.

A very sensitive inner hearing registers this when the mountain spirit strides across the mountains.

It is a subtle sway and a vibration that comes from the inside of the mountain. If it assumes a shape, the mountain spirit decorates itself with the rare flowers and grasses- that the mountain, that is, the stones and the soil, produce. Now and then it wears a crown on its head. It is similar to the jags and peaks of the mountains. When nature beings and the mountain spirit meet, they greet each other in a very friendly fashion and are devoted to one another in love. However, the majesty of the mountains is not always open for a conversation.

The mountain spirit is very anxious to have everything take place in an orderly way on the mountains and that the mountains stay clean. It does not like the disorder of human beings, who leave paper and other things lying about in the mountains.

When people act against the laws of the mountains, against the Order, then the mountain spirit puts its consciousness to work, so that they leave its territory. It then calls the air spirit, for example, and asks it to blow a cold and stormy wind or to drive clouds toward the mountain so that a rain shower comes. It asks the animals to indicate with their behavior that the weather is changing, so that the mountaineer or mountain hikers can recognize this.

The mountain spirit also grumbles when people climb the mountains or go for a walk in the mountains inattentively or with thoughts loaded with problems. It stomps with its foot against a mountain peak, so that the vibration causes a thunder-like noise and the people, afraid that a thunderstorm is approaching, then return to the valley.

So, when you visit the mountains, try to take the mountain spirit seriously. Greet this elemental energy and strive not to be engrossed in sullen and gloomy thoughts. Otherwise, the mountain spirit will send out its energies, stream into your thoughts and, for some reason or another, cause you not to want to climb the mountain at all.

The mountain spirit is a very bizarre elemental spirit. Its nature still corresponds to the craggy and massive rocks. However, it is also very friendly and loving. It can rejoice like a small child when people come to it and delight in the mountain, in the massive rocks, the beauty of the mountain meadows and the individual flowers or refresh themselves at the small and larger springs that flow from inside the mountain.

The mountain spirit is happy when people are pure in their thoughts. The disposition, the power of love of the mighty giant, of the mountain spirit, can become like that of a child. In its childlike joy, the spiritual shape, the mountain spirit, then goes deeper into the valley than usual, in order to draw closer to these people. It radiates its sensations of love into the sunny disposition of the mountain climber or hiker and leads them to sunny or shady places. By way of its world of sensations, it tells people to look here and there, either into the valley or up to the mountain summit on which the sun is shining. It shows friendly hikers a rare flower or a beautiful stone and even prompts them to take it with them. If the mountain climbers or hikers want to take the stone and put it thankfully into their pocket, the mighty giant, the mountain spirit, increases the positive powers of the stone, which then also have a positive effect on the particular person.

These powers of the stones, of these small gifts from the mountain spirit, stimulate people to further positive thinking; or they remind them again and again of the beautiful world of the mountains, when they have difficulties or when they are tired from the burden of their daily life.

The positive powers also have an effect on the magnetic field of the people who have the stone and they stabilize their nervous system. However, the effect of the stone depends on the composition of the minerals and trace elements that it contains; for these form its consciousness. This has an effect on the person, especially when the mountain spirit has increased its positive powers.

Thus, dear brothers and sisters, you recognize that the language of the pure beings is one of pure, light-filled sensations. They communicate with light-filled people via their pure sensations. Often, you do not sense or know that these are the powers of love of the pure beings or of the elemental spirits.

But the mountain spirit reacts angrily when a person picks a whole bouquet of rare flowers in order to put them in a vase at home. Then it is possible that the mountain spirit withdraws the spiritual life of the flowers, so that either they are already wilted when the mountain climber or hiker arrives home or that they wilt quickly in the vase. However, it gladly gives a hiker a single flower as a gift.

It also leads good people to springs and encourages them to drink, while increasing the positive powers of the water, so that they become healing forces. These then benefit the body, refreshing, building it up and strengthening it.

When a good person, a hiker, takes a break, breathes deeply and wipes the perspiration from his brow, the mountain spirit calls the air spirit and asks it to let cool air flow toward the hiker. If the hiker then feels well and strengthened and is happy with the cool breath of air, the giant mountain spirit is even more joyful. The great giant hops around like a child and thanks the All-Spirit that good people have perceived it and it could serve them.

However, sometimes it can also be very stern with the elves and the gnomes, when they don't keep everything on the reserve the way it thinks is good. However, it also readily lets itself be taught by the nature beings, for it knows that these have a more developed consciousness than it does.

The mountain spirit is very happy – you, dear brothers and sisters, would say that it is an enthusiast – when the elemental beings, the fire and air spirits, the elves and gnomes have their prayer dance, the sun dance. Then sometimes it puts itself into the middle of the circle and lets the small elves lovingly stroke its beard and hair, which consist of fine grasses and stems. The mountain spirit then laughs like a child. If it laughs loudly, it echoes over the whole mountain range. Then many small animals come to the prayer dance and sing a quiet song for the mountain spirit.

When at nightfall the animals and flowers go to rest and the elemental beings go back to their spiritual homes, the mountain spirit then sits on a mountain peak to receive the last rays of the setting sun and the first rays of the new rising sun. Or the mighty spiritual shape, the form, dissolves and flows as energy deep into the mountain.

And so, dear brothers and sisters, you realize that everything that you step on is alive. Everywhere, wherever you are, you are surrounded by visible and invisible life.

God's All-power is in fire, in the air, in water and in the stone.

God's All-power is in the animal, in the plant, in the bush and in every tree.

God's All-power is in the elves and the dwarfs.

God's All-power is in every mountain.

God's All-power is also in you and in every person who is your neighbor.

God's All-power is active in every soul, in a guardian angel, in all Being.

Anyone who loves God loves the visible and invisible life.

Anyone who loves selflessly does not ask about being at home. They recognize: Neither here nor there, there is no place anywhere where God is not. Thus, everywhere is eternity, also in the earthly garment. That is truly being at home.

Anyone who loves God doesn't seek one place where God could be; God is omnipresent, everywhere. God is consciousness. He is all in all things. He is also in you, that is, very near! He is here. Wherever you are, God is there.

Dear brother, dear sister, you say you cannot see Him. But you behold God's All-power in the stone, in the plant, in the animal and in the stars. You behold God's All-power in your neighbor and in yourself.

> Live in God and find the good in all Being,
> then joy, love, peace and harmony
> draw into your soul.
> And you remain happy and glad
> and your neighbor, as well.

I wish for you the sun in your hearts. Radiate it out!
It is God's love. Carry it from house to house.

Love, serve, remain selfless, as you are from the very beginning. Then, with many, you will change this world and there will be light.

I greet you with the peace of the homeland
and extend my hand to you.
I extend it to you from the spiritual garment.
Accept it and go with me hand in hand,
into the land of love,
for God is love.

Peace!

Your spiritual sister *Liobani*

LIOBANI:
I Explain –
Will You Join Me?
(12 - 18 years)

Liobani helps young people to find freedom in God and to take their life into their hands, for example:

How do I find out what my type is, or what my abilities are? What profession is the right one for me? How do I deal with the difficulties I have in life, for example, with my parents? Is there such a thing as love at first sight? ... and much more.

Contents:

The day is your friend: The Energy of the Day • Find the positive in all negativity • Intellect and Intelligence • The consciousness in you, the Inner Helper and Advisor • Occupational choice and occupational life – Our attitude toward work and income • The choice of your life's companion – external or internal values, what attracts you? • The spiritual ethical principles for a good marriage and partnership • The inner life is expressed externally: Home and clothing ... and much more.

208 pp., SB, Order No. S 130en, ISBN: 978-1-890841-66-9

We will be happy to send you our current catalog as well as free reading samples to many topics.

Gabriele Publishing House – The Word
P.O. Box 2221, Deering, NH 03244, USA
Toll Free No. 001-844-576-0937
International: +49.151.1883.843
www.gabriele-publishing-house.com